The New Golden Dictionary

by Bertha Morris Parker

Illustrated by Aurelius Battaglia

A GOLDEN BOOK, NEW YORK
Western Publishing Company, Inc.
Racine, Wisconsin 53404

A a

The first letter of the alphabet

about

Daddy is reading
a story **about** a duck.
It is **about** time
to go to bed.
It is nearly time
to go to bed.

above

The airplane is **above** the clouds.
The clouds are **above** the town.

accident

The cars had an **accident**.

Paul had an **accident**
with his milk.

acrobat

An **acrobat** can do
tricks.
We see **acrobats**
at the circus.

across

Mark hopped **across** the room
on one foot.

Eric lives
across the street from Mark.

act (acts / acted / acting)

The children
are **acting** out a story.
They are playing
they are bears.
Sandy **acts** as if
he wants to help.

address

Ann knows her **address**.
She can tell
where she lives.

afraid

Little children
are sometimes **afraid**
of big dogs.

after

Sue will not eat her candy
till **after** lunch.

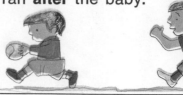

Bobby ran **after** the baby.

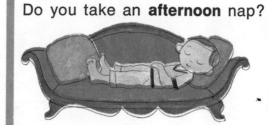

afternoon

Afternoon is after the clock
says noon.
Do you take an **afternoon** nap?

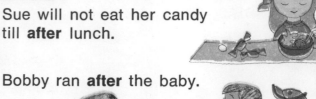

again

John said to Daddy,
"Do it **again**."
John wants Daddy
to lift him once more.
He likes to be lifted
again and **again**.

against

The ladder is leaning
against the wall.

David and Jim are playing
against Mike and Tony.

a b c d e f g h i j k l m

4

ago

Children played with these toys a long time **ago**.

air

Fresh **air** is coming in the window. We breathe **air**. **Air** covers the whole earth.

airplane

An **airplane** is a machine that flies.

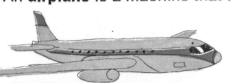

Airplanes carry people. They carry mail and many other things.

airport

An airplane is taking off from the **airport**. Airplanes land at **airports** too.

alike

The two red shapes are **alike**.

The yellow shapes are not **alike**.

alive

These are **alive**.

These are not **alive**. Are you **alive**?

alligator

An **alligator** is a big animal with thick skin.

almost

Almost means nearly. Nine pennies **almost** make a dime.

alone

Lisa is **alone**. Nobody is with her.

along

Jane's mother said, "Come **along** to the store with me. There are things to see **along** the way."

alphabet

The **alphabet** has 26 letters. Polly knows the **alphabet**.

always

The light is **always** on. It is on all the time.

Ken **always** hits the ball. He hits it every time.

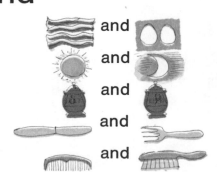

and

 and

and

and

and

and

n o p q r s t u v w x y z

animals

These are all **animals**.
There are many,
many more kinds.

cow and calf

butterfly and cocoon

bullfrog and tadpole

clam

skunk

fly

koala

raccoon

starfish

spider

bear and cub

earthworm

octopus

goat and kid

jackrabbit

jellyfish

opossum

lobster

horse and colt

pigeon

dolphin

lizard

deer and fawn

flamingo

hippopotamus

duck and duckling

queen conch

rattlesnake

beaver

salmon

porcupine

a b c d e f g h i j k l m

6

ankle

Touch one of your **ankles**.
Bend the **ankle**.

another

Pam wants
another cookie.
She already has
one cookie.

answer (answers / answered / answering)

Daddy **answered**
the telephone.

"What has an eye
but can't see?"
Do you know the **answer**
to this riddle?

answer
A NEEDLE

ant

An **ant** is an insect.
Most **ants** live
in the ground.

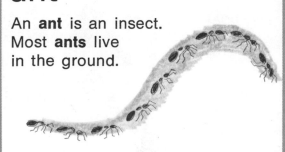

any

Johnny doesn't want
any more.

anyone

Can **anyone** jump
as high as the moon?
No, nobody can.

anything

Barbara will eat **anything**
her mother puts on her plate.
She likes any kind of food.

apartment

This **apartment**
is Bill's home.
It is in
a big **apartment** building.

ape

An **ape** has long arms
and no tail.
Apes can stand and
walk on two feet.

apple

An **apple** is a fruit.
Apples grow on trees.
Apples are red or
green or yellow.

April

April is a month.
Some years
Easter comes
in **April**.

apron

An **apron** keeps clothes
clean.
These are all **aprons**.

aquarium

An **aquarium** is a bowl or tank
for fish to live in.
A building with many kinds
of fish to look at
is an **aquarium** too.

arm

Tom has one **arm** up.

Debby is sitting on the **arm** of Daddy's chair.

around

The hands of the clock go **around** in a circle.

The squirrels ran **around** the tree.

arrow

An **arrow** for a bow is a thin pointed stick.

Signs that point the way to go are **arrows** too.

ask (asks / asked / asking)

Susan **asked** Joan to come over and play.
Karen is going to **ask** Santa Claus for crayons.
Timmy is always **asking** why.

asleep

Rachel is **asleep**.

astronaut

An **astronaut** rides out in space.
Some **astronauts** have been to the moon.

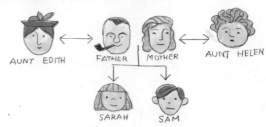

at

Jerry and Jennifer are **at** the museum.
Jerry is looking **at** a dinosaur.
Jennifer is looking **at** the clock.
Their bus leaves **at** noon.

August

August is a month.
August comes after July.

aunt

Sarah and Sam have two **aunts**.
Aunt Helen is their mother's sister.
Aunt Edith is their father's sister.

automobile

One **automobile** has a good place for pets.
Automobiles are often called cars.

awake

Sharon is **awake**.
She is not asleep.

away

The boat is far **away**.

Ned threw **away** his broken toy.

a b c d e f g h i j k l m

B b

The second letter of the alphabet

baby

A very young child is a **baby.**

Very young animals are called **babies** too.

back (backs / backed / backing)

Daddy **backed** the car into the parking place.

Skipper is bringing **back** the ball.

You cannot see your **back.**

Chairs have **backs.**

bad

Bad means not good. Is Fluff being **bad**? It was a **bad** day for a picnic.

bag

A **bag** is used for carrying things.

bake (bakes / baked / baking)

We **bake** food in an oven. Biscuits are **baking** in the oven.

ball

A **ball** is fun to throw and to catch.

Lots of games are played with a **ball.**

Are these **balls** to play with?

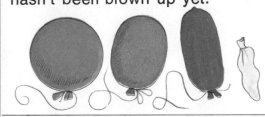

balloon

Here are four **balloons.** One **balloon** hasn't been blown up yet.

banana

A **banana** is a fruit. Ripe **bananas** are yellow outside and white inside.

band

A **band** plays music.

A rubber **band** is holding on the lid.

bandage

Tom has a **bandage** on his finger.

bang

A **bang** is a loud noise.

bank

A **bank** is a place to keep money.

bar

One candy **bar** has nuts in it.

There are **bars** at the window.

bark

Tree trunks are covered with **bark**.

bark (barks / barked / barking)

The little dog **barks** a lot.
His **bark** is loud.

barn

A **barn** is a building on a farm.
Cows live in this **barn**.

baseball

Baseball is a game.
The players use a ball and a bat.
We call the ball a **baseball** too.

basket

Baskets are used for holding things.

Here are a **basket** of strawberries

and a **basket** of flowers

and a **basket** of clothes.

basketball

Basketball is a game.
The boys are playing **basketball**.
The ball is called a **basketball** too.

bat (bats / batted / batting)

In a baseball game you **bat** the ball with a baseball **bat**.

bat

A **bat** is a small furry animal that flies.

Do you think **bats** look like mice with wings?

bath

Taking a **bath** makes you clean.

bathing suit

You wear a **bathing suit** to go wading or swimming.

beach

The **beach** is sandy.

bead

Here is a string of **beads**.

Each **bead** has a small hole for the string.

bean

A **bean** is a vegetable.
There are many kinds of **beans**.

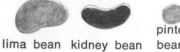 

lima bean   kidney bean   pinto bean   string bean

a **b** c d e f g h i j k l m

bear

Bears are big furry animals with short tails.
Have you ever seen a **bear** at the zoo?

beard

This man has a red **beard**.

beat (beats / beat / beaten / beating)

Jack is **beating** a drum.

Mother is **beating** an egg.

Gordy is **beating** Sara in a race.

beautiful

Very pretty things are **beautiful**.
We like to look at them.
We like to listen to **beautiful** music too.

because

Sammy cannot see the store window **because** he is too little.

bed

We sleep in a **bed**.
Betsy goes to **bed** for her nap.

bee

A **bee** is an insect.
Bees make honey.

honey-bee   bumblebee

beetle

A **beetle** is an insect.
These are all **beetles**.

June beetle   tumblebug

caterpillar hunter   ladybug   beetle   firefly

before

Christmas Eve is the night **before** Christmas.

Benjy found two eggs **before** Jane found any.

A comes **before** B.

begin (begins / began / begun / beginning)

It is **beginning** to rain.

The baby **began** to cry.

Ben's name **begins** with B.

behind

Susan is **behind** Jimmy.
Spotty is **behind** Susan.

What is **behind** the tree?

believe (believes / believed / believing)

Do you **believe** in fairies?
Do you think there are fairies?

Daddy **believes** a bad storm is coming.

bell

Bells ring.
Find the **bell** on the red car.

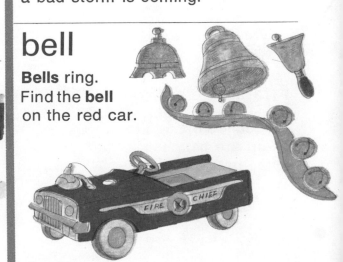

n o p q r s t u v w x y z

11

belong
(belongs / belonged / belonging)

The red boots **belong** to George.
They are George's boots.

The book **belongs** on the shelf.
It goes on the shelf.

below

Jane lives on the floor **below** John.
Jake lives on the floor **below** Jane.

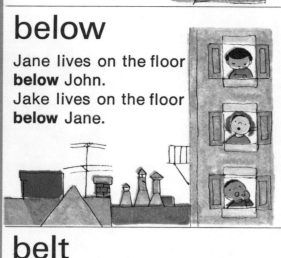

belt

Julie's **belt** is blue.
Jeff and Joel have brown **belts**.

bench

A **bench** is a place to sit.
There are **benches** in the park.

bend
(bends / bent / bending)

Bend down and touch your toes.

The tree **bent** in the wind.

beside

The spoon is **beside** the dish.

The cat is **beside** the kitten.

best

Dan is Bobby's **best** friend.

What story do you like **best**?

better

Janet skates **better** than June.
She is a **better** skater.

Which do you like **better** — peanuts or popcorn?

between

The children are sitting **between** their mother and father.
The girl is **between** the two boys.

bicycle

A **bicycle** has two wheels.
Bicycles are not all alike.

big

The little boy has a **big** book.
His **big** brother has a little book.

bill

The robin has a cherry in its **bill**.

robin

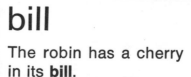

What do the other birds have in their **bills**?

cuckoo   grosbeak

heron

a **b** c d e f g h i j k l m

birds

A **bird** is an animal with feathers. Most **birds** can fly.

red-winged blackbird

nighthawk

starling

gull

wren

crow

blue jay

screech owl

purple martin

sandpiper

Baltimore oriole

meadowlark

pelican

roadrunner

loon

ostrich

cockatoo

swan

scarlet tanager

mockingbird

redstart

penguin

kingfisher

chimney swift

flicker

birthday

Your **birthday** comes at the same time every year.

When is your **birthday**?

bit

A **bit** of something is not very much. Here are some **bits** of paper and string.

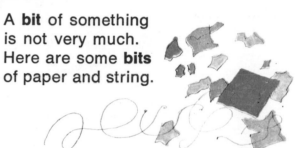

bite (bites / bit / bitten / biting)

Did a mosquito ever **bite** you?

Someone took a **bite** of the cookie and a **bite** of the apple.

black

Coal is **black**.

The cat is **black**.

The pretty bowl is **black**.

n o p q r s t u v w x y z

13

blade

Scissors have two **blades** to cut with.

A **blade** of grass is one leaf of grass.

blanket

A **blanket** is a warm cover. These children have **blankets** over them.

block

Ben is building a tower with his **blocks**.

This **block** has a tall building at one end and a playground at the other end.

blood

There is **blood** inside your body. When you get hurt, you may see some of your **blood.**

blow (blows / blew / blown / blowing)

Is the wind **blowing**?

Jenny **blew** up the balloon.

blue

Blue is a color.

Here are a **blue** cap,

a **blue** flower,

and a **blue** kite in a **blue** sky.

blueberry

A **blueberry** is a fruit. **Blueberries** grow on **blueberry** bushes.

bluebird

A **bluebird** has a sweet song. The baby **bluebirds** are hungry.

board

A **board** is a flat piece of wood. Many things are made of **boards**.

boat

A **boat** is for riding on the water. Here are three kinds of **boats**.

body

Your **body** is all of you from the top of your head to the tips of your toes.

All animals have **bodies**.

bone

There are **bones** inside your body. A **bone** is hard.

Shep has a toy **bone**.

book

The **book** is
on the table.

Some **books** have
stories and pictures
in them.

boot

Boots are for feet.

Can you find the **boot**
Charles is looking for?

both

Both girls
are eating popcorn.

Both the calf and
the pony have spots.

bottle

The baby drinks milk
from a **bottle**.

Here are
some other **bottles**.

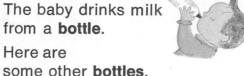

bottom

The puppy is
at the **bottom** of the ladder.
A kitten is at the top.

bounce (bounces / bounced / bouncing)

This ball **bounces**.
It hits the sidewalk
and comes up again.
Can you **bounce** a ball?

bow

There is a yellow **bow**
on the package.

Some hunters hunt
with **bows** and arrows.

box

One of the **boxes**
holds crayons.

One has breakfast food
in it.

What could be
in the other **box**?

boy

Here are three **boys**.
Think of a name for each **boy**.

bracelet

Beth has a **bracelet.**
She wears it
on her arm.

branch

A **branch** is part
of a tree.
A big tree has
many **branches**.

n o p q r s t u v w x y z

brave

A fireman is **brave**.
There is danger
in fighting fires.

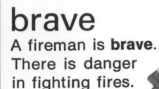

Helen is **brave**.
She didn't cry
when she was lost.

bread

Bread is good to eat.
Do you like **bread**
with jelly on it?

break (breaks / broke / broken / breaking)

The plate **broke**
when Sue dropped it.

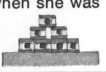

A kite string
may **break** in the wind.

The pencil is **broken**.

breakfast

Mary eats **breakfast**
at eight o'clock
every morning.
What do you like
for **breakfast**?

breathe (breathes / breathed / breathing)

You **breathe** air in.
Then you **breathe** air out.
Most of the time
you **breathe**
through your nose.

brick

A **brick** is hard.
Many buildings
are built of **bricks**.

bridge

You can see two **bridges**
over the river.
Cars are going across one **bridge**.
The other **bridge** is for trains.

bright

The sun is very **bright**.

Lamps are **bright** too.

bring (brings / brought / bringing)

Mother asked Nan
to **bring** the plates.

David is **bringing**
a chair.

What has Pal **brought**?

brook

A **brook** is a tiny river.

broom

Brooms are used
for sweeping.
Penny sweeps
the kitchen floor
with her toy **broom**.

brother

Don is Pat's **brother**.
Don and Pat have
the same mother and father.

Brothers often
look alike.

a **b** c d e f g h i j k l m

16

brown

Brown is a color.
Here are a **brown** bird

and a **brown** bear
and a **brown** beard.

brush (brushes / brushed / brushing)

Amy **brushed** her hair.

Find the **brush**
for **brushing** teeth.

bubble

A **bubble** is round.
It is filled with air.
Bubbles break
if you touch them.

bucket

Daddy carries water
in the **bucket**.
He needs many **buckets**
of water
to wash
the car.

bud

This **bud** will open
into a rose.

bug

A **bug** is an insect.
These are all **bugs**.

giant waterbug

squash bug   stinkbug   milkweed bug

buggy

Susie is giving
her doll a ride
in her doll **buggy**.

Before there were cars
many people had **buggies**
to ride in.

build (builds / built / building)

Birds **build** nests.

The children
are **building**
a sand castle.

Men **built**
this skyscraper.

buildings

There are many kinds
of **buildings**.
Here are some
of the different kinds.

apartment house   fire engine
house   school

gas station

movie theater

tower

Catholic church   Protestant
church

synagogue

factory

stadium

office building

state capitol

one-story house

bulb

A light **bulb** gives light.

A tulip **bulb** grows into a tulip.

bump (bumps / bumped / bumping)

Mike fell and **bumped** his head. He fell and hit his head. There was a **bump** in the sidewalk.

bun

Do you like a hamburger on a **bun**?

Hot dogs are good on **buns** too.

bunch

Here are a **bunch** of keys and a **bunch** of flowers and two **bunches** of grapes.

bunny

Bunny is another word for rabbit.

burn (burns / burned or burnt / burning)

A fire is **burning** in the fireplace.

Paper **burns**. The toast was **burned**.

Mother said, "The soup is hot. Don't **burn** your tongue."

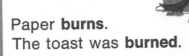

bus

A **bus** is a big car with lots of seats. **Buses** stop here to let people on and off.

bush

A **bush** is a plant. These **bushes** have pretty flowers.

busy

Mother is **busy**. She has lots to do.

but

The kitten is small **but** not small enough to follow the mouse.

All the B's **but** one are facing the right way.

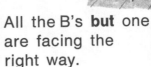

BBBℬB

butter (butters / buttered / buttering)

Butter is a food.

Martha is **buttering** the toast.

buttercup

Buttercups are shiny yellow flowers.

butterfly

A **butterfly** is an insect. Here are three **butterflies**.

monarch butterfly   sulphur butterfly   black swallowtail

a b c d e f g h i j k l m

button (buttons / buttoned / buttoning)

Joan was **buttoning** her coat.

A **button** came off. How many **buttons** are left?

Pushing the **button** will bring the elevator.

buy (buys / bought / buying)

Gus is **buying** candy. He pays the man a dime. Then the candy belongs to Gus.

by

Alan is standing **by** the corner mailbox. A truck in going **by**. The truck is driven **by** Alan's uncle.

C c
The third letter of the alphabet

cabbage

Cabbage is a vegetable. **Cabbages** are balls of leaves as round as your head.

cage

A **cage** has wires or bars for walls. The little **cage** is for a bird.

The big **cage** is for monkeys.

cake

A **cake** is sweet. **Cakes** are baked in ovens.

call (calls / called / calling)

Mother is **calling** the children home.

Andy **calls** his baby brother Bubby.

camel

A **camel** is a large, strong animal. Some **camels** have two humps.

camp (camps / camped / camping)

Roy's family is **camping** near a lake.

Steve goes to **camp** every summer.

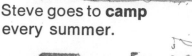

can

Cans are made to hold things.

What is in this **can**?

canary

A **canary** is a bird with a beautiful song. **Canaries** often live in cages.

n o p q r s t u v w x y z

19

candle

A **candle** is burned to give light.

candy

Candy is made with sugar.

Almost everybody likes **candy.**

cap

A **cap** is a cover for the head.

Some bottles have **caps.**

car

A **car** moves on wheels. Automobiles are **cars** used on streets and roads.

Railroad **cars** move on tracks.

card

Ruth got a birthday **card** in the mail.

Games with **cards** are good for rainy days.

cardinal

Another name for a **cardinal** is redbird. **Cardinals** have a loud, sweet song.

care

Ann is taking **care** of her little sister.

careful

Everyone is **careful** not to wake the baby.

carpet

The floor is covered with **carpet.**

carrot

A **carrot** is a vegetable. We eat **carrots** raw or cooked.

carry (carries / carried / carrying)

Daddy **carried** in the packages.

This mother animal **carries** her babies on her back.

cart

David is helping to push the **cart.**

castle

This is a **castle** of long ago.

cat

A **cat** is a small furry animal. **Cats** are good pets.

a b **c** d e f g h i j k l m

catch (catches / caught / catching)

Jody will **catch** the ball.

Jean's cat **caught** a mouse yesterday.

Al is **catching** cold.

caterpillar

A **caterpillar** looks like a worm. Some **caterpillars** are baby butterflies. Some are baby moths.

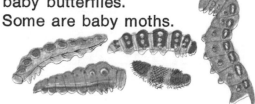

cave

A **cave** is a big hole under the ground. **Caves** are not safe places to play.

cent

A **cent** is a piece of money. A **cent** is the same as a penny.

center

The **center** is the middle.

A doughnut has a hole in the **center**.

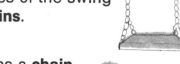

chain

Silky's collar is a **chain**.

The sides of the swing are **chains**.

Clare has a **chain** she wears around her neck.

chair

A **chair** has a back. Some **chairs** have arms.

chalk

Greg is drawing a picture with **chalk**.

Elsa used **chalk** to make these lines.

change (changes / changed / changing)

Jerry **changes** his clothes after school.

Ed **changed** seats with Tom.

Karen paid for her milk with a dime. She got back five cents **change**.

chase (chases / chased / chasing)

Mary's kitten **chases** its tail.

cheek

Bill's **cheeks** are red.

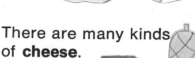

cheese

Cheese is made from milk.

There are many kinds of **cheese**.

n o p q r s t u v w x y z

cherry

A **cherry** is
a small red fruit.
Cherries grow on trees.

chest

Put your hand
on your **chest**.

A **chest** is a big box with a lid.
Guess what is in this **chest**.

chicken

A **chicken** is a bird
used for food.
We eat **chicken** eggs
too.

child (children)

You are a **child**.
Some **children** are boys.
Some are girls.

chimney

A **chimney** carries away
smoke.

Some factories have
tall **chimneys**.

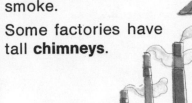

chin

Your **chin** is part
of your face.

Santa's beard hides
his **chin**.

chipmunk

A **chipmunk** is
a small furry animal.
Chipmunks carry food
in their cheeks.

chocolate

These foods are made
with **chocolate**.
Pick out the ones
you like.

choose (chooses / chose / chosen / choosing)

Today was Alice's turn
to **choose** a TV show
to watch.
She **chose** a cowboy show.
She picked out a cowboy show.

Christmas

Christmas is a day
of loving and giving.

Christmas is
the birthday of Jesus.

Christmas tree

Lights and
other pretty things
are hung
on a **Christmas tree**.

circle

This is a **circle**.

To play the game
the children made a **circle**.

Rings are **circles**.

a b c d e f g h i j k l m

circus

A **circus** is a big show. In a **circus** we see animals that do tricks. We see funny clowns. We see acrobats too at **circuses**.

city

Lots of people live and work in **cities**. A **city** has many streets and many buildings.

clap (claps / clapped / clapping)

In patty-cake we **clap** our hands.

Daddy **clapped** to show he liked the play.

claw

An animal's sharp toenail is called a **claw**.

A kitten's **claws** are little but they can scratch you.

clay

The children made animals out of **clay**.

clean (cleans / cleaned / cleaning)

Father is **cleaning** the garage.

Mike's face is **clean**. He just washed it.

clear (clears / cleared / clearing)

Timmy is **clearing** away the snow.

The water is **clear**. It is easy to see the stones at the bottom.

climb (climbs / climbed / climbing)

Bert is **climbing** a tree.

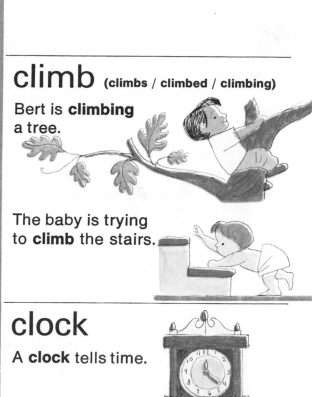

The baby is trying to **climb** the stairs.

clock

A **clock** tells time.

close (closes / closed / closing)

Nicky can **close** the door. He can shut the door.

Try **closing** first one eye and then the other.

cloth

These are rolls of **cloth**.

Most clothes are made of **cloth**.

Daddy has a **cloth** to shine his shoes.

clothes

Clothes are things to wear.

baby's bonnet

bedroom slippers

nightgown

pants

poncho

scarf

snowsuit

blouse

dress

skirt

sweater

T-shirt

underwear

coast (coasts / coasted / coasting)

Dan is **coasting**.
Dan is sliding
downhill.

coat

We wear **coats**
over our other clothes.

A mother rabbit pulls
hair from her **coat**
of fur to make a nest.

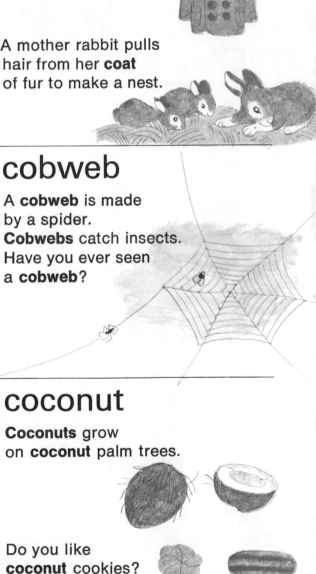

cloud

There is a big **cloud**
in the sky.
Clouds can shut out
the sun.

clown

A **clown** tries
to make people laugh.
There are **clowns**
in a circus.

cobweb

A **cobweb** is made
by a spider.
Cobwebs catch insects.
Have you ever seen
a **cobweb**?

clover

Clover is a plant
with pretty flowers.
Have you ever found
a four-leaf **clover**?

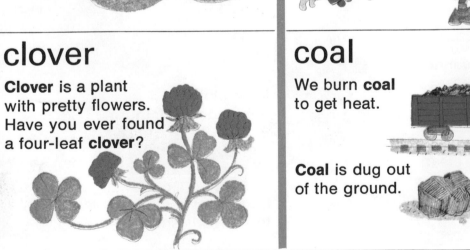

coal

We burn **coal**
to get heat.

Coal is dug out
of the ground.

coconut

Coconuts grow
on **coconut** palm trees.

Do you like
coconut cookies?

a b c d e f g h i j k l m

coffee

Coffee is a drink
many grown-ups like.

cold

Cold means not warm.
Sean would be **cold**
without his snowsuit.
Patty has a bad **cold**.

color (colors / colored / coloring)

Penny is **coloring** a picture.

Point to the **color**
you like best.

comb (combs / combed / combing)

Julie is **combing**
her hair. Her **comb**
is red.

come (comes / came / coming)

"Here, Sport, **come** here."
Sport **came**
when Marty called.

company

Company is coming
for dinner.

cook (cooks / cooked / cooking)

It's time to **cook**
the dinner.
Mother is **cooking** it.

Men make
good **cooks** too.

cookie

A **cookie** is good
to eat.
These are all **cookies**.

cool

Cool means not very cold.
Do you wear a sweater on a **cool** day?

corn

Corn is a vegetable.
Corn is a grain too.

Many animals eat **corn**.

corner

The ball rolled
into the **corner**.

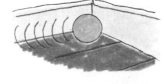

The table has
sharp **corners**.

Shep waits
at the **corner** for Tony
to say "Go."

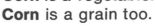

cost (costs / cost / costing)

A piece of the candy **costs** a penny.

cotton

Cotton comes from **cotton** plants.

Some clothes are made of **cotton** cloth.

cough (coughs / coughed / coughing)

Mother comes when she hears the baby **coughing**.
Reuben **coughs** a lot.
He has a bad **cough**.

count (counts / counted / counting)

Barbara is **counting** her crayons.
She is finding out how many she has.

Sam can **count** to one hundred.

country

The land outside of towns and cities is in the **country**.
Farms are in the **country**.

The United States is a **country**.

cousin

Children of your aunts and uncles are your **cousins**.
How many **cousins** do you have?

cover (covers / covered / covering)

Joe's boots are **covered** with mud.

Mother is **covering** the baby.

Do you pull up the **covers** when you get cold at night?

cow

A **cow** gives milk.
Cows are farm animals.

cowboy

Cowboys ride horses.
The **cowboy** is chasing a calf.

crack (cracks / cracked / cracking)

The glass **cracked** when the picture fell.

Squirrels **crack** nuts.

Cathy jumped over the **crack**.

cracker

A **cracker** is thin and dry.
Crackers are good with soup.
Some **crackers** are sweet.

crawl (crawls / crawled / crawling)

Ted **crawled** under the bed to get his ball.

Caterpillars **crawl**.

a b **c** d e f g h i j k l m

26

crayon

Crayons are good
for making pictures.
Cindy used
a green **crayon** for the grass.

cream

Mother puts **cream**
in her coffee.
A cow's milk has
cream in it.

crib

A **crib** is a baby's bed.
The sides keep
the baby from falling out.

crooked

The street is **crooked**.
It is not straight.
Draw a **crooked** line.

cross (crosses / crossed / crossing)

Ben **crossed** the street.
He walked
to the other side.

Can you **cross**
your fingers?

There is a **cross**
on the church.

crossing guard

A **crossing guard** helps
school children cross
the street safely.

crowd (crowds / crowded / crowding)

There are many people
in a **crowd**.
The store is **crowded**.

crown

A **crown** is worn
on the head.
Many **crowns** are gold.
Kings and queens have
crowns.

crumb

Crumbs are tiny bits
of dry food.
Bread and crackers and
cookies leave **crumbs**.
Do you ever put out
bread **crumbs**
for the birds?

cry (cries / cried / crying)

Children **cry** when
they get hurt.
The baby is **crying**
because he is hungry.

cup

Do you drink your milk
from a **cup**?
Most **cups** have handles.

cupboard

A **cupboard** has shelves.
Kitchen **cupboards** are
for pans and dishes
and food.

n o p q r s t u v w x y z

cupcake

A **cupcake** is a little cake. **Cupcakes** are often baked in paper cups.

curl (curls / curled / curling)

The kitten is **curled** up in Susan's chair.

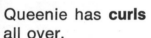

Josie has a **curl** on the top of her head.

Queenie has **curls** all over.

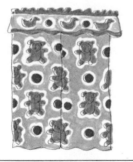

curtain

The window has **curtains**. They keep out the light.

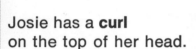

cut (cuts / cut / cutting)

Martha is **cutting** out a paper doll.

Terry **cut** his finger.

The baby **cut** a tooth this morning.

D d

The fourth letter of the alphabet

daddy

Children often call their father **Daddy**.

dance (dances / danced / dancing)

Sue likes to **dance**. She is **dancing** to music.

dandelion

A **dandelion** is a weed with pretty flowers. Did you ever blow away **dandelion** seeds?

danger

A **danger** sign means "Be careful or you may get hurt."

dark

Dark means not light. It is **dark** at night.

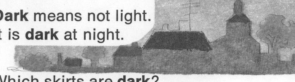

Which skirts are **dark**?

daughter

A girl is the **daughter** of her mother and father. This mother and father have three **daughters**.

day

It is light during the **day**. Can you name the **days** of the week?

dear

We often call people we love **dear**. Most letters begin with **Dear**.

a b c d e f g h i j k l m

December

December is a month. Christmas comes in **December**.

deep

There is **deep** water by the diving board. The water is not **deep** in the wading pool.

dentist

Dentists take care of people's teeth. Jeff is at the **dentist's**.

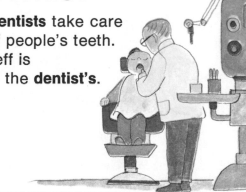

desert

A **desert** is land that is very dry. In some **deserts** people ride camels.

desk

Bill is writing at his **desk** at school.

These **desks** are in a big office.

dew

Some mornings the grass is wet with **dew**. A drop of **dew** is a tiny drop of water.

dictionary

A **dictionary** is a book about words.

different

One car is **different** from the others. It is not like the others.

Which caterpillar is **different**?

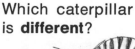

dig (digs / dug / digging)

Joe is **digging** in the sand. He found a little clam in the sand he **dug** up.

dime

Dimes are money. A **dime** is as much as ten pennies.

dinner

Sometimes we have **dinner** at noon. Sometimes we have **dinner** in the evening. Cindy likes her **dinner**.

dirt

Sam has been rolling downhill in the **dirt**. He is **dirty** all over.

n o p q r s t u v w x y z

dish

Skipper has his own **dish**.

Bowls and cups and plates are **dishes**.

dive (dives / dived or dove / diving)

Eddie **dived** into the water. It was a good **dive**.

divide (divides / divided / dividing)

Jane **divided** the candy. She gave some to Terry and some to Ruth. She kept the rest.

doctor

A **doctor** helps make sick people well. **Doctors** help people stay well too.

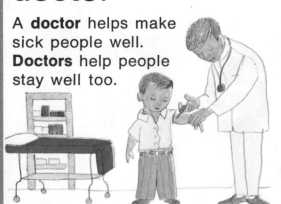

dog

A **dog** is a good pet. Some **dogs** are big when they grow up. Some are little.

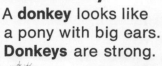

doll

The **dolls** are going for a ride. One **doll** has eyes that open and shut.

dollar

A **dollar** is money. A hundred pennies make a **dollar**.

dollhouse

Ann is putting a rug in her **dollhouse**.

donkey

A **donkey** looks like a pony with big ears. **Donkeys** are strong.

door

We go in and out through **doors**. The **door** is opening.

doughnut

A **doughnut** is a small fried cake.

down

The leaves floated **down** to the ground.

The boys ran **down** the street.

downstairs

Betty is coming **downstairs**.

a b c **d** e f g h i j k l m

30

dozen

Here are a **dozen** eggs.
A **dozen** means twelve.

draw (draws / drew / drawn / drawing)

Cal likes to **draw**.
What has he **drawn**?

drawer

The bottom **drawer**
is Katie's.

dream (dreams / dreamed or dreamt / dreaming)

Willie **dreamed**
he was a giant.
He liked his **dream**.

dress (dresses / dressed / dressing)

Pat can **dress** himself.
Mary **dressed** her doll
in the new **dress**.

drink (drinks / drank / drunk / drinking)

Jim **drank** four glasses
of milk yesterday.

Nora is getting
a **drink** at the fountain.

drive (drives / drove / driven / driving)

Betsy's aunt **drives**
the school bus.

drop (drops / dropped / dropping)

Timmy is **dropping**
in a quarter.

The baby likes
to **drop** his bottle.

Drops of rain
are falling.

drum

John can play
the **drum**.
You can march
to the sound
of a **drum**.

dry (dries / dried / drying)

Mother is **drying**
Wendy's hair.

The clothes are **dry**.

duck

A **duck** is a bird
that can swim and fly.
Wild **ducks** fly south
in the fall.

during

Pam went to sleep
during the TV show.

dust (dusts / dusted / dusting)

Nancy is **dusting**.
She wipes off the **dust**
with a cloth.

dwarf

There are **dwarfs**
in some fairy stories.
A **dwarf** is someone
very small.

n o p q r s t u · v w x y z

E e

The fifth letter of the alphabet

each

The twins look like **each** other.

Each girl has a hat.

eagle

An **eagle** is a large bird. **Eagles** have strong wings and bills and claws.

ear

Your **ears** are for hearing.

An **ear** of corn is good to eat.

early

In summer the sun comes up **early** in the morning. It comes up before you are awake.

The eight o'clock bus is **early**. It is ahead of time.

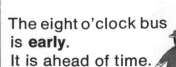

earth

The **earth** is big and round.

Plants grow in **earth**.

east

Dick is looking north. His right hand is pointing **east**. The sun comes up in the **east**.

Easter

Easter is a holiday that comes in the spring. **Easter** is always on Sunday.

easy

It is **easy** for the cat to climb the tree. It is not **easy** for Jim.

eat (eats / ate / eaten / eating)

The children **eat** lunch at noon. They are **eating** hot dogs.

edge

Lee is walking along the **edge** of the sidewalk.

The blanket has blue **edges**.

egg

An **egg** is easy to cook.

All birds hatch from **eggs**.

eight

8

Eight tells how many. Here are **eight** jacks

and **eight** marbles.

A daddy longlegs has **eight** legs.

a b c d e f g h i j k l m

elbow

Your arm bends at the **elbow**.

Tommy has worn holes in the **elbows** of his sweater.

electric

Here are an **electric** lamp and

an **electric** iron and

an **electric** toaster.

elephant

An **elephant** has a long trunk. The **elephants** at the circus marched around in a circle.

elevator

An **elevator** takes people up and down. Tall buildings have **elevators**.

eleven

Eleven tells how many. Here are **eleven** birthday candles

11

and **eleven** lollipops.

elf (elves)

An **elf** is a little fairy. **Elves** in fairy stories often play tricks.

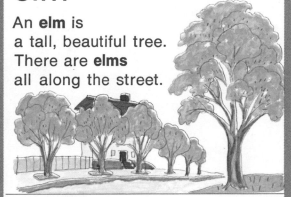

elm

An **elm** is a tall, beautiful tree. There are **elms** all along the street.

empty

The cookie jar is **empty**. There is nothing in it.

end (ends / ended / ending)

The TV show **ends** at 8 o'clock. It is over at 8 o'clock.

The caboose is at the **end** of the train. It is the last car.

engine

An **engine** is a machine. Cars have **engines**. This big **engine** pulls a train.

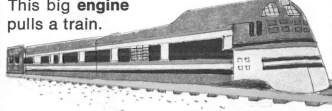

enough

Andy is not tall **enough** to ring the doorbell. Susan has **enough** money to buy a coloring book.

envelope

Connie put her letter in an **envelope**.

n o p q r s t u v w x y z

escalator

Escalators are stairs that move. You stand still on an **escalator** step.

even

Emmy is small. Stevie is **even** smaller.

evening

In the **evening** it begins to get dark.

ever

Did you **ever** see anything like this?

every

Don and Angie go to the playground **every** day.

A bell rings **every** time the ball goes in.

everybody

Everybody is waving. All the people are waving.

everything

Curt picked up **everything** he had been playing with.

excuse (excuses / excused / excusing)

It is polite to say "**Excuse** me" when you bump into someone.

eye

Your **eyes** are for seeing.

Hans has blue **eyes**. Vic's **eyes** are brown.

The thread goes through the **eye** of the needle.

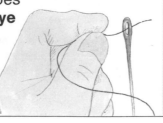

F f

The sixth letter of the alphabet

face

To see your **face** you look in a mirror. Does Ben's **face** always look the same?

factory

A **factory** is a place where things are made. Lucy's father works in a shoe **factory**.

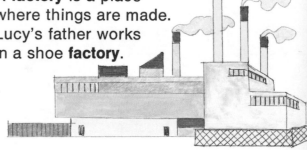

fair

Henry went to the **fair**. At **fairs** there are lots of things to see and do.

fairy

Fairies are only in stories. They are not real people. The book is a **fairy** story.

a b c d e f g h i j k l m

34

fall (falls / fell / fallen / falling)

A coconut is **falling**.

The doll **fell** over.

Fall is part of the year.
It comes between summer
and winter.

family

There are five people
in Tim's **family**.
How many are there
in your **family**?

fan (fans / fanned / fanning)

Tina is **fanning**
herself.

Fans make us cooler.

far

Chuck lives
far from the beach.
He lives a long way
from the beach.

farm

A **farm** is a place
for raising animals
and plants.
Most of our food comes
from **farms**.

farmer

A **farmer** runs a farm.
What are
these **farmers** doing?

fast

Don ran **fast**.
He got to the fence
in a hurry.

The top is spinning **fast**.

fasten (fastens / fastened / fastening)

Carol **fastens**
her seat belt
in the car.

Bert is **fastening**
the engine
to the coal car.

fat

One pig is **fat**.
The other pig is thin.

Find the **fat** mouse.

father

Here is Bill's **father**.
He is
Betty's **father** too.
Bill and Betty are
his children.
Daddy is
another name
for **father**.

feather

Birds have **feathers**.
A **feather** is soft
and light.

February

February is a month.
Valentine's Day comes
in **February**.

n o p q r s t u v w x y z

feed (feeds / fed / feeding)

Adam **feeds** his dog
every day.
He gives food
to his dog.

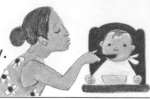

Mother
is **feeding** Amy.

feel (feels / felt / feeling)

Glass **feels** smooth.

Fur **feels** soft.

Ice **feels** cold.

Ann has been sick.
Now she is **feeling**
better.

fence

The **fence** keeps
the horses in the field.

few

Few means not many.
Here are a **few** roses
and many violets.

field

A **field** is a piece
of land.
One of these **fields**
is used for corn.
The other one
is a football **field**.

fight (fights / fought / fighting)

The cat and dog
are **fighting**.

Children sometimes
have **fights**.

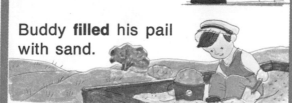

fill (fills / filled / filling)

Mary is **filling**
a glass with milk.

Buddy **filled** his pail
with sand.

find (finds / found / finding)

Frank **found** the letters
of his name in his soup.

Can you **find**
Kate's belt for her?

finger

Someone put a **finger**
in the bowl.

Jenny is painting
with her **fingers**.

finish (finishes / finished / finishing)

Mother **finished**
the story.
She read to the end
of the story.

fire

A **fire** is very hot
and bright.
In **fires** something
burns.

fire engine

A **fire engine** is coming
down the street.
Fire engines go fast.

a b c d e **f** g h i j k l m

fireman (firemen)

A **fireman** puts out fires. The **firemen** are using a hose.

fireplace

A fire in a **fireplace** warms a room.

Fireplaces outdoors are for cooking.

first

Jean is **first** in line.

The big turtle finished the race **first**. It won **first** prize.

fish (fishes / fished / fishing)

The boys are **fishing**. They are trying to catch some **fish**.

Fish live in water.

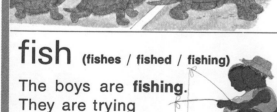

five

Five tells how many. Here are **five** flies

and **five** flowers

and **five** little foxes.

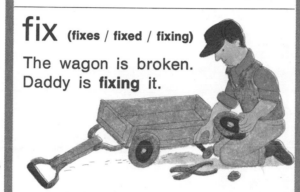

fix (fixes / fixed / fixing)

The wagon is broken. Daddy is **fixing** it.

flag

The **flag** has red and white stripes. What other color is in the **flag**?

flashlight

We carry **flashlights** to help us see in the dark.

flat

The top of the table is **flat**.

The sidewalk and

the floor are **flat** too.

float (floats / floated / floating)

The toy duck **floats** on the water.

Some balloons **float** in the air.

floor

These **floors** are made of boards.

Guess who made the tracks on this kitchen **floor**.

flour

Mother uses **flour** to make a cake. Bread is made from **flour** too. Most **flour** comes from wheat.

flowers

Many plants have **flowers**.

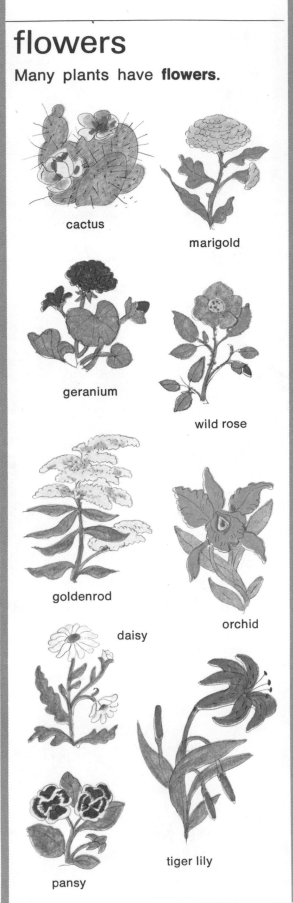

cactus

marigold

geranium

wild rose

goldenrod

orchid

daisy

pansy

tiger lily

fly (flies / flew / flown / flying)

Most birds can **fly**.

A jet plane **flew** over the house.

Mario is **flying** a toy airplane.

A **fly** is an insect.

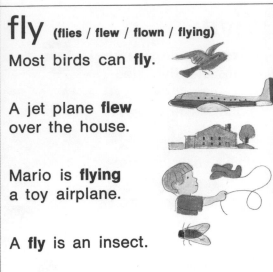

fog

A **fog** is a cloud near the ground. It is hard to see in thick **fogs**.

fold (folds / folded / folding)

Mother is **folding** up a blanket.

Tad **folded** the paper.

follow (follows / followed / following)

The geese are **following** Mary.
They are going along behind her.

Ken's little brother **follows** Ken everywhere.

food

We eat many kinds of **food**. Here are some of them.

beef stew

butter

biscuit

celery

cheese

cherries

chili

chocolate cake

corned beef hash

chocolate pudding

chop suey

roast chicken

French fries

grits

milk

orange juice

pancakes

potato chips

prunes

apple salad

sardines

sausage

steak

tomato

strawberry shortcake

ham sandwich

a b c d e **f** g h i j k l m

foot (feet)

You have five toes on each **foot**.

The squirrel is at the **foot** of the tree.

There are twelve inches in a **foot**.

football

These boys are playing **football**. The ball is called a **football** too.

for

Larry paid a dime **for** a ball.
The ball was **for** his sister.
It is time **for** lunch.
Norma set the table **for** Mother.
Grandfather went **for** a walk.
He walked in the park **for** an hour.

forehead

Your **forehead** is a part of your face.

forest

In a **forest** there are many trees. The trees grow close together in **forests**.

forget (forgets / forgot / forgotten / forgetting)

Micky **forgot** his cap. He did not think to take it with him.

fork

Arthur is eating his supper with a **fork**.

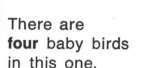

fountain

Here are two **fountains**. One is to drink from. The other **fountain** is pretty to look at and listen to.

four

Four tells how many.

There are **four** robin eggs in this nest.

There are **four** baby birds in this one.

Fourth of July

The **Fourth of July** is a holiday. It is our country's birthday.

fox

A **fox** looks like a dog. **Foxes** are wild animals.

free

Ellie got a **free** ride on the merry-go-round. She didn't have to pay for it.

One bird is in a cage. The other bird is **free**.

n o p q r s t u v w x y z

freeze
(freezes / froze / frozen / freezing)

Water **freezes**
when it is very cold.
It turns to ice.
Mother says, "Put on
your mittens or
your hands will **freeze**."
She means your hands
will feel too cold.

fresh

The flowers are **fresh**.
Ida just picked them.
The carrots are **fresh**
too.

Friday

Friday is a day
of the week.
Friday comes
after Thursday.

friend

Pam and Lisa
are **friends**.
They like
each other.

frog

A **frog** is
a small animal.
Frogs live in water
till they grow up.

from

Jean ran
from the window
to the door.

Her brother is coming
home **from** school.
He has a duck
he made **from** clay.

front

The engine is at the **front**
of the train.

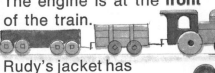

Rudy's jacket has
a zipper down the **front**.

Val is in **front** of Ed.

frost

Windows may
have **frost**
on them in winter.
Sometimes we say
Jack **Frost** painted them.

fruit

Fruit is good to eat.
Which kinds of **fruit**
do you like best?

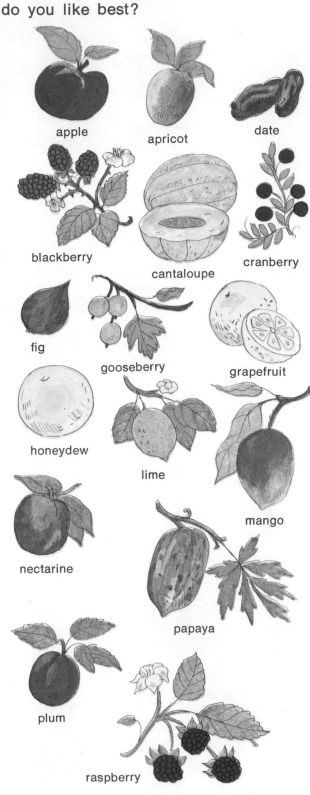

apple

apricot

date

blackberry

cantaloupe

cranberry

fig

gooseberry

grapefruit

honeydew

lime

mango

nectarine

papaya

plum

raspberry

a b c d e **f** g h i j k l m

full

The cup is **full**
of lemonade.
What will happen if
Gail pours more in?

fun

Neil has **fun** playing
with his dog.

The girls
are having **fun**
jumping rope.

funny

The children are seeing
a **funny** show.
How do you know
it is **funny**?

fur

Fur is
the soft, thick hair
that covers
some animals.

Elsa has a coat
that looks like **fur**.

furniture

Most rooms have
furniture.
All these things
are **furniture**.

armchair

floor lamp

chest of drawers

clothes hamper

garbage can

umbrella stand

dishwasher

globe

hassock

dinette table and chairs

sofa

record player

rocking chair

twin beds

stool

bookcase

magazine rack

flower cart

wastebasket

n o p q r s t u v w x y z

G g

The seventh letter of the alphabet

games

We play **games** for fun. What **game** do you like best?

blind-man's buff

tick-tack-toe

checkers

hopscotch

card game

ping-pong

magnet fish-pond game

garage

A **garage** is a place to keep a car. There are big **garages** for parking and fixing cars.

garbage

Scott threw the wormy apple in the **garbage**. The big truck will carry the **garbage** away.

garden

Gardens are places where flowers and vegetables grow.

gas

Gas is burned for cooking and for heating. We cannot see the **gas** if it is not burning.

The **gas** that makes cars run looks like water.

gate

A **gate** is like a door. It lets you go through a fence or a wall.

get (gets / got / getting)

It's time to **get** up.
Lee **gets** sleepy early.
Sandra **got** new shoes yesterday.
Mother is **getting** dinner.

ghost

Pete dressed like a **ghost** on Halloween.

giant

There are **giants** in some fairy stories. A **giant** is someone very big and tall.

a b c d e f **g** h i j k l m

giraffe

A **giraffe** has a very long neck and many spots. **Giraffes** are the tallest animals in the world.

girl

Here are three **girls**. Think of a name for each **girl**.

give (gives / gave / given / giving)

Timmy said, "Please **give** me some." Chuck **gave** Timmy some of his popcorn.

glad

Becky's dog is **glad** to see her. His tail shows how **glad** he is.

glass

We can see through most **glass**. **Glass** breaks.

Find the drinking **glass**.

Find the **glasses** that help people see better.

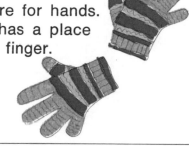

glove

Gloves are for hands. A **glove** has a place for each finger.

go (goes / went / gone / going)

Dan said, "**Go** home, Tuffy!" Tuffy **went**.

goat

A **goat** is a lot like a sheep. **Goat's** milk is good to drink.

gold

Gold is a yellow metal. These things are **gold**. Can you tell what each one is?

goldfish

Goldfish are good pets. Most **goldfish** are the color of gold, but some are not.

good

Ice cream tastes **good**. Milk is **good** for us.

Ida is reading a **good** book.

Is Pepper being **good**?

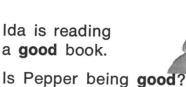

good-by

Mother and Daddy are going to a show. Wendy is waving **good-by**.

n o p q r s t u v w x y z

goose (geese)

A **goose** is a big bird that can swim. Wild **geese** fly south in the fall.

grain

We call the seeds of some plants **grain**. Rice, corn, and wheat are **grains**.

Butch had **grains** of sand in his shoes.

grandfather

Here are Fred's father's father and his mother's father. They are his **grandfathers**.

grandmother

Here are Fred's father's mother and his mother's mother. They are his **grandmothers**.

grape

A **grape** is a small fruit. **Grapes** grow in bunches on vines.

grass

Grass is a plant with long, narrow leaves. **Grass** makes a soft green carpet on the ground.

grasshopper

A **grasshopper** is an insect. **Grasshoppers** have long, strong back legs good for hopping.

great

The giant in the story lived in a **great** castle.

A **great**-grandmother is a grandmother's mother or a grandfather's mother.

green

Green is a color.

Here are a **green** light

and a **green** leaf and

a little **green** apple.

grocery store

Irma is at the **grocery store**. She is buying crackers, apples, and a can of soup for lunch.

ground

Harry can jump down to the **ground**.

The plants are growing in the **ground**.

group

A **group** has more than one in it. Here are two **groups** of children playing.

a b c d e f **g** h i j k l m

44

grow (grows / grew / grown / growing)

Kiku **grew** a lot last year.
She has **grown** too big for her coat.

guess (guesses / guessed / guessing)

Frank doesn't know what is in the box.
He **guesses** that it is a space helmet.
What is your **guess**?

guitar

A **guitar** makes music.
Guitars have strings.

guppy

A **guppy** is a tiny fish.
Guppies are good pets.

Hh
The eighth letter of the alphabet

hair

Hair grows on our heads.

Many animals have **hair** all over.

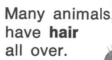

half (halves)

These things have been cut in **half.**
They have been cut in two.
The two **halves** of anything are the same size.

Halloween

Children like to dress up on **Halloween.**
They ring doorbells.
Halloween is the last day of October.

hamburger

A **hamburger** is a cooked patty of meat.
Hamburgers make good sandwiches.

hammer (hammers / hammered / hammering)

Father **hammered** the nails into the wood.
A **hammer** is a tool.

hand (hands / handed / handing)

Margie **handed** Rita the red crayon.

You have four fingers and a thumb on each **hand.**

The **hands** of a clock point to the time.

handkerchief

A **handkerchief** is a square piece of cloth.
Handkerchiefs are good for wiping your eyes or your nose.

handle

A **handle** is for holding something with your hand.

n o p q r s t u v w x y z

hang (hangs / hung / hanging)

Abe is **hanging** by his hands.

Abbie **hung** her coat in the closet.

Hanukkah

Hanukkah is a happy time for Jewish people. **Hanukkah** comes in December.

happen (happens / happened / happening)

Brenda wonders what will **happen** next in the story.

What is **happening** here?

happy

Nora is **happy.** She feels glad about something. Can you guess what?

hard

These things are **hard.** They are not soft.

It is **hard** to learn to skate. Tim had a **hard** bump.

hat

Marcy's **hat** ties under the chin. There are lots of kinds of **hats.**

hatch (hatches / hatched / hatching)

The mother hen sat on the eggs to **hatch** them.

have (has / had / having)

You **have** a dictionary. Will **has** one too. Benjy is **having** a nap. Marcia **had** to go home.

hay

Hay is dried grass. Some farm animals eat **hay.**

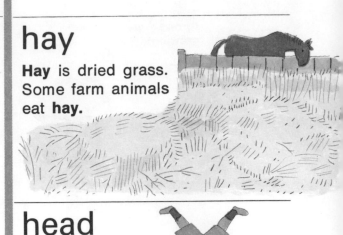

head

Gus can stand on his **head.**

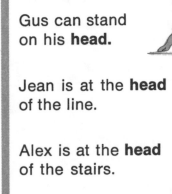

Jean is at the **head** of the line.

Alex is at the **head** of the stairs.

hear (hears /heard / hearing)

Peg **hears** something under the steps.

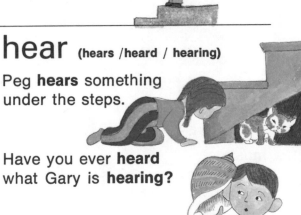

Have you ever **heard** what Gary is **hearing?**

heart

Your **heart** is in your chest. When you run, you can feel it beating.

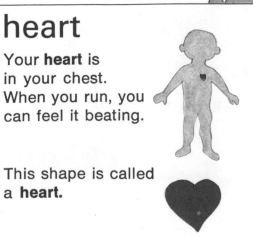

This shape is called a **heart.**

heat (heats / heated / heating)

Mother is **heating** the soup.
Fire gives off **heat**.

heavy

The book is too **heavy** for Barry.
It weighs too much.

heel

You have two **heels**.
Each of your socks has a **heel** too.
Most shoes have **heels**.

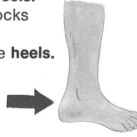

helicopter

Helicopters are much like airplanes.
Does a **helicopter** have wings?

hello

Rosa said **hello** to the new girl.
She was being friendly.

helmet

Helmets are something like hats.

Pat's football **helmet** keeps his head from getting hurt.

help (helps / helped / helping)

Sid is **helping** with the leaves.
Daddy says he is a big **help**.

hen

A **hen** lays eggs.
Some grown-up chickens are **hens**.
Some are roosters.

hide (hides / hid / hidden / hiding)

Tony is **hiding** under the table.

Max **hid** his crayons from his little brother.

high

The swing is too **high** for Kim.

Rockets go **high** above the earth.

hill

A **hill** is high ground.
You can see a long way from the top of a **hill**.

hit (hits / hit / hitting)

Frank **hit** his head.
Can you see how?

Have you ever heard rain **hitting** the roof?

n o p q r s t u v w x y z

hold (holds / held / holding)

Alan will **hold** the baby.

Daddy's car **holds** five people.

Jennifer's mother says, "**Hold** still!"

hole

The sock has a **hole** in it.
Some animals live in **holes** in the ground.

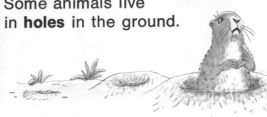

holiday

A **holiday** is a day to have fun.
Thanksgiving and Christmas are **holidays**.
Do you know any others?

hollow

These things are **hollow**.
Hollow things have space inside them.

homes

The place you live in is your **home**.
Do any of these **homes** look like yours?

adobe house

apartment house

houseboat

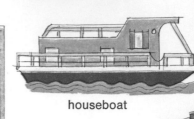

thatched cottage

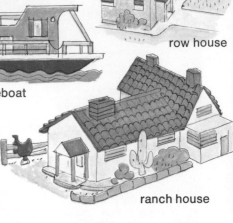

row house

ranch house

brick house

house on stilts

mobile home

igloo

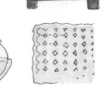

farmhouse

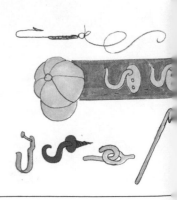

tepee

honey

Bees make **honey**.
Honey is very sweet.
Do you like bread and **honey**?

hook

This **hook** is for catching fish.

We hang coats and caps on **hooks**.

Here are some other **hooks**.

a b c d e f g **h** i j k l m

hoop

A **hoop** is a big ring.

The dolphins are jumping through **hoops.**

hop (hops / hopped / hopping)

A grasshopper **hops.**
Toads and robins and rabbits **hop.**
Can you **hop** on one foot?

horn

Some animals have **horns.**

This kind of **horn** makes a noise when you blow it. Automobiles have **horns.**

horse

Many people ride **horses.**

A race **horse** goes fast.

Some **horses** pull wagons.

hose

Water for the grass is running through the **hose.**

Firemen use **hoses.**

hospital

A **hospital** is a place with beds for sick people. Doctors and nurses work in **hospitals.**

Many babies are born in **hospitals.**

hot

The iron is **hot.**
It could burn you.

In summer the sun feels **hot.**

hot dog

A **hot dog** is made of meat.
We eat **hot dogs** for lunch or supper or on picnics.

hotel

A **hotel** is a place where people away from home can sleep and eat.

hour

An **hour** is 60 minutes long.
Each day of the week has 24 **hours.**
The little hand of the clock is the **hour** hand.

house

This **house** is June's home.
Only June's family lives in it.

how

Many questions start with **how.**
How are you?
How hot is it?
Laura is learning **how** to swim.

hug (hugs / hugged / hugging)

Vern is **hugging** his toy bear. Caroline gave her baby sister a big **hug**.

hummingbird

A **hummingbird** is the smallest bird there is.

hump

The camel has a **hump**. Buffaloes have **humps** too.

hundred

A **hundred** is a big number. Here are a **hundred** tiny beads.

100

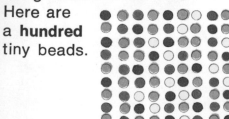

hungry

The twins are **hungry**. They want their supper.

hunt (hunts / hunted / hunting)

Pearl is **hunting** for her milk money. Maggie is helping her **hunt**.

hurry (hurries / hurried / hurrying)

Henry is **hurrying** home. He is going fast. Henry is always in a **hurry** for his lunch.

hurt (hurts / hurt / hurting)

Sandy has **hurt** his paw. It **hurts** when he walks on it.

hydrant

The **hydrant** is near the street. Firemen get water from **hydrants** to put out fires.

I i

The ninth letter of the alphabet

ice

The **ice** is from a refrigerator. **Ice** is frozen water.

ice cream

Do you like **ice cream**? **Ice cream** has milk and sugar in it.

ice cream cone

Debby is eating an **ice cream cone**. She will have to hurry. The **ice cream** is melting.

ice skates

Ice skates are for skating on ice. When you are just learning to skate, you may fall down a lot.

a b c d e f g **h** **i** j k l m

icicle

An **icicle** is made of ice.
Water running
off a roof may freeze
and make **icicles**.

in

There is a white mouse
in the cage.

Count the fish
in the aquarium.

inch

We measure
some things in **inches**.
The line is
an **inch** long.
Shirley measured
the book
with a ruler.
The ruler showed
it was 10 **inches**
wide.

ink

Shirley wrote
her name in **ink**.
She wrote it
in green **ink**.
She used a pen.

insects

Insects are small animals
with six legs.
All these are **insects**.

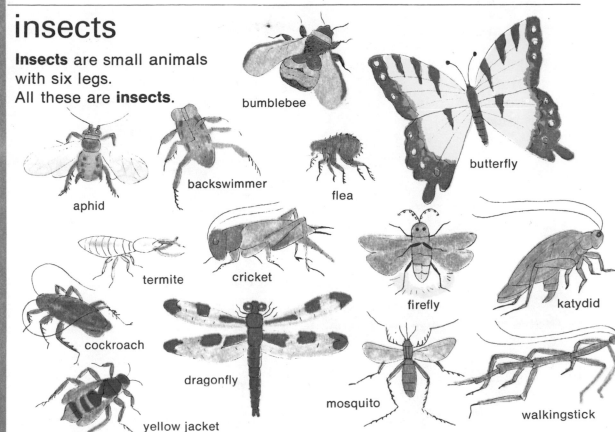

bumblebee

butterfly

aphid

backswimmer

flea

termite

cricket

firefly

katydid

cockroach

dragonfly

mosquito

walkingstick

yellow jacket

inside

Can you see what is
inside the box?
Can you see what is
inside the sack?

invite (invites / invited / inviting)

Sally is **inviting** Archie
and Anne to a party.
She is asking them
to come to a party.

iron (irons / ironed / ironing)

Jimmy's mother
is **ironing** Jimmy's shirt.
She is using
an electric **iron**.
Iron is a metal.

island

Ida made a picture
of an **island**.
Islands have water
all around them.

J j

The tenth letter of the alphabet

jacket

A **jacket** is
a short coat.
Both boys and girls
wear **jackets.**

jack-in-the-box

A **jack-in-the-box** is
a toy.
Open the box.
Up jumps Jack.

jack-o'-lantern

A **jack-o'-lantern**
is made out of a pumpkin.
We make **jack-o'-lanterns**
for Halloween.

jacks

Jacks is a game.
You play it
with **jacks.**
You use a ball too.

jam

Jam is sweet.
Jams are made of fruit
and sugar.

January

January is a month.
It is the first month
in the year.

jar

A **jar** is for holding
things.
Most **jars** are glass.

jelly

Jelly is made
from fruit juice
and sugar.

jellyfish

A **jellyfish** is
a water animal.
It hasn't any head
or tail or legs.

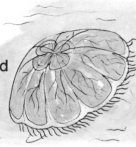

jet plane

Jet planes fly fast.
Hot gases come
from their engines.

joke

A **joke** is something
funny.
June is playing
a **joke** on Kate.

jolly

Jolly people laugh and
tell funny stories.
They make
other people happy.

juice

We can squeeze **juice**
from most fruits
and vegetables.
Many people drink
juice at breakfast.

orange juice

tomato juice

grapefruit juice

a b c d e f g h i j k l m

July

July is a month.
July comes
after June.

jump (jumps / jumped / jumping)

Bobby is holding
a stick for Rags
to **jump** over.
Bobby's sister
is **jumping** rope.
Jim made a long **jump.**

June

June is a month.
June comes
after May.

just

The little train
is **just** starting to go.

Supper is **just** about
ready.
The shoes are **just**
the right size for Joe.

K k

The eleventh letter of the alphabet

kangaroo

A **kangaroo** is
a big furry animal.
Kangaroos hop about.
A mother **kangaroo**
carries her baby
in a pocket.

keep (keeps / kept / keeping)

Do you **keep**
the pretty leaves you find?
Here is a good way
of **keeping** leaves.

key

Mother carries a bunch
of **keys**.
One **key** is for the lock
on the front door.

kick (kicks / kicked / kicking)

Sammy can **kick**
a football a long way.
He just **kicked**
the ball over the fence.

kind

An ant is one **kind** of insect.
There are many other **kinds**.

Jody is **kind**
to his little sister.

kindergarten

Some children start
school in **kindergarten**.
In **kindergarten**
they work and play
with other children.

king

A **king** is the ruler
of a country.
Kings sometimes wear
crowns.

kiss (kisses / kissed / kissing)

Carlotta is **kissing**
her father good-by.

Margie is giving
her doll a **kiss**.

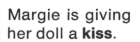

n o p q r s t u v w x y z

kitchen

A **kitchen** is a room for cooking.
Kitchens always have stoves and sinks.

kite

Did you ever fly a **kite**?
Sometimes **kites** go high in the air.

kitten

A **kitten** is a baby cat.
Kittens like to play.

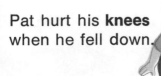

knee

Point to your **knee**.

Pat hurt his **knees** when he fell down.

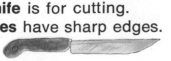

knife (knives)

A **knife** is for cutting.
Knives have sharp edges.

knit (knits / knitted / knitting)

The woman is **knitting** a sweater.
She **knitted** a bonnet yesterday.

knock (knocks / knocked / knocking)

Knock this toy over and up it comes.

The kitten **knocked** over the blocks.

Lucy is **knocking** on the door.

knot

Jerry tied a **knot** in the string.
The **knot** keeps the string in place around the box.

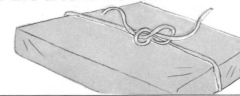

know (knows / knew / known / knowing)

Do you **know** your address?
Cal **knows** his.
He **knew** it when he got lost.

L l

The twelfth letter of the alphabet

lace

Lace is sometimes sewn on clothes.

Some shoes have **laces**.

ladder

Ladders are something like stairs.
A **ladder** can be moved to the place where we want to climb up.

lake

A **lake** has land all around it.
At **lakes** people swim and fish and ride in boats.

lamb

A **lamb** is a baby sheep.

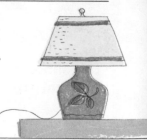

lamp

A **lamp** gives off light.

a b c d e f g h i j **k** l m

land (lands / landed / landing)

The airplane is **landing** at the airport.

Some parts of the earth are **land**. Other parts are water.

lap

Can Laura hold Rags on her **lap**?

large

Large means big. Pick out the **large** ball

and the **large** bell

and the **large** bill.

last

Butch took the **last** apple. There are no apples left.

Jean is **last** in line. **Last** time she was first.

last (lasts / lasted / lasting)

The show **lasted** an hour. It was an hour long.

late

Charlie is **late** for dinner again. Everyone else was on time.

laugh (laughs / laughed / laughing)

Chris is **laughing** at something funny. He has a loud **laugh**.

laundry

Clothes to be washed go in the **laundry**. Some people send dirty clothes to **laundries**.

lay (lays / laid / laying)

The hen has **laid** an egg. She **lays** one every day. **Lay** one hand on top of the other.

lazy

The cat is **lazy**. It is too **lazy** to chase the mouse.

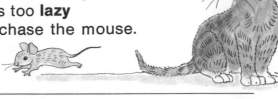

lead (leads / led / leading)

Gene is **leading** Star to the barn. He **leads** and Star follows.

leaf (leaves)

A **leaf** is part of a plant. Most **leaves** are green.

lean (leans / leaned / leaning)

Ken hurt his ankle. He is **leaning** on Bert.

Helen **leaned** over to see the fish.

n o p q r s t u v w x y z

learn (learns / learned / learning)

Ralph has **learned** to tie his shoes.

Dora is **learning** to play jacks.

leather

Many shoes are made of **leather**.
Leather comes from the skin of animals.

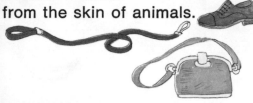

leave (leaves / left / leaving)

Zeke's family is **leaving** for a vacation.
Daddy sometimes forgets and **leaves** the car lights on.
Kay **left** her mittens at home.

left

Maria is holding up her left hand.

Now Maria is holding up her **left** foot too.

leg

We stand and move about on our two **legs**.

How many **legs** do these animals have?

lemon

A **lemon** is a fruit.
Lemons are sour.

let (lets / let / letting)

Bruce **let** the dog out.
Mother sometimes **lets** Rosa stay up late.
Marty is **letting** some air out of the balloon.

letter

We make words out of **letters**.
What **letter** does your name begin with?

The mailman brings **letters**.

library

A **library** is a place where books are kept.
Some **libraries** let us take books home to read.

lick (licks / licked / licking)

Tabby **licks** her kittens to get them clean.

Margie is **licking** her lollipop.

lid

A **lid** is a cover.
Pans and chests and boxes have **lids**.

Your eyes have **lids** too.

lie

Ned broke a cup and said he did not do it.
Ned told a **lie**.

a b c d e f g h i j k l m

lie (lies / lay / lain / lying)

The children are **lying** in the shade.
Spot **lay** there for a while too.

lift (lifts / lifted / lifting)

Father **lifted** Doris high in the air.

light

It is **light** during the day.
The **light** comes from the sun.

Electric **lights** help us see at night.

light

These things are **light**.
They are not heavy.
They are easy to lift.

lightning

In some storms we see **lightning** in the sky.

like (likes / liked / liking)

Eric **likes** orange juice for breakfast.
Daddy **likes** tomato juice.

like

Linda's dress is almost **like** Joy's.

line

Katie drew a red **line.**
A **line** of cars waited for the train to go by.

Daddy got a knot in his fishing **line.**

lion

A **lion** is a big wild animal.
There are **lions** at the zoo.

lips

Your **lips** help you talk.
Can you say "five fat puppies" without using your **lips?**

listen (listens / listened / listening)

The children are **listening** to music.
They have to be quiet to **listen.**

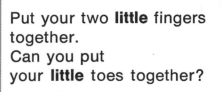

little

Mario's dog is **little**.

Put your two **little** fingers together.
Can you put your **little** toes together?

live (lives / lived / living)

Sheila **lives** on a farm.
Dinosaurs **lived** long ago.
Some of them **lived** on plants.
They ate plants.

n o p q r s t u v w x y z

57

load (loads / loaded / loading)

Mother **loaded**
the car with children.

Brad has a big **load.**

loaf (loaves)

Here are two **loaves**
of white bread and
one **loaf** of dark bread.

lock (locks / locked / locking)

We **lock** a door
by turning the key
in the **lock.**
When the door
is **locked,** no one
can open it.

lollipop

A **lollipop** is a piece
of hard candy
on a stick.

long

Wendy's hair is **long.**

A kangaroo makes
long hops.

It rained
all day **long.**

look (looks / looked / looking)

Jeff said,
"**Look** at the parachute."

Abe called, "**Look** out!
A car is coming!"

Nan is **looking** for Peg.
Jill is **looking** after
her little sister.

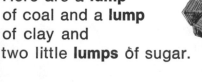

lose (loses / lost / losing)

Beth has **lost** a button.
Val's kitten was **lost,**
but Val found her.
Doug's side is **losing**
the game.

loud

The music is too **loud.**
Say your name out **loud.**

love (loves / loved / loving)

The people in this family
love each other.
Love makes people happy.

low

Ginnie is
on a **low** bar.
Dan has climbed
up high.

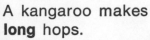

lump

Here are a **lump**
of coal and a **lump**
of clay and
two little **lumps** of sugar.

Guess why the boy has
a **lump** in his cheek.

lunch

Emily takes her **lunch**
to school.
She eats **lunch** at noon.

Mother is packing
a picnic **lunch.**

a b c d e f g h i j k l m

M m

The 13th letter of the alphabet

machines

These are **machines**.
A **machine** helps us
get work done.

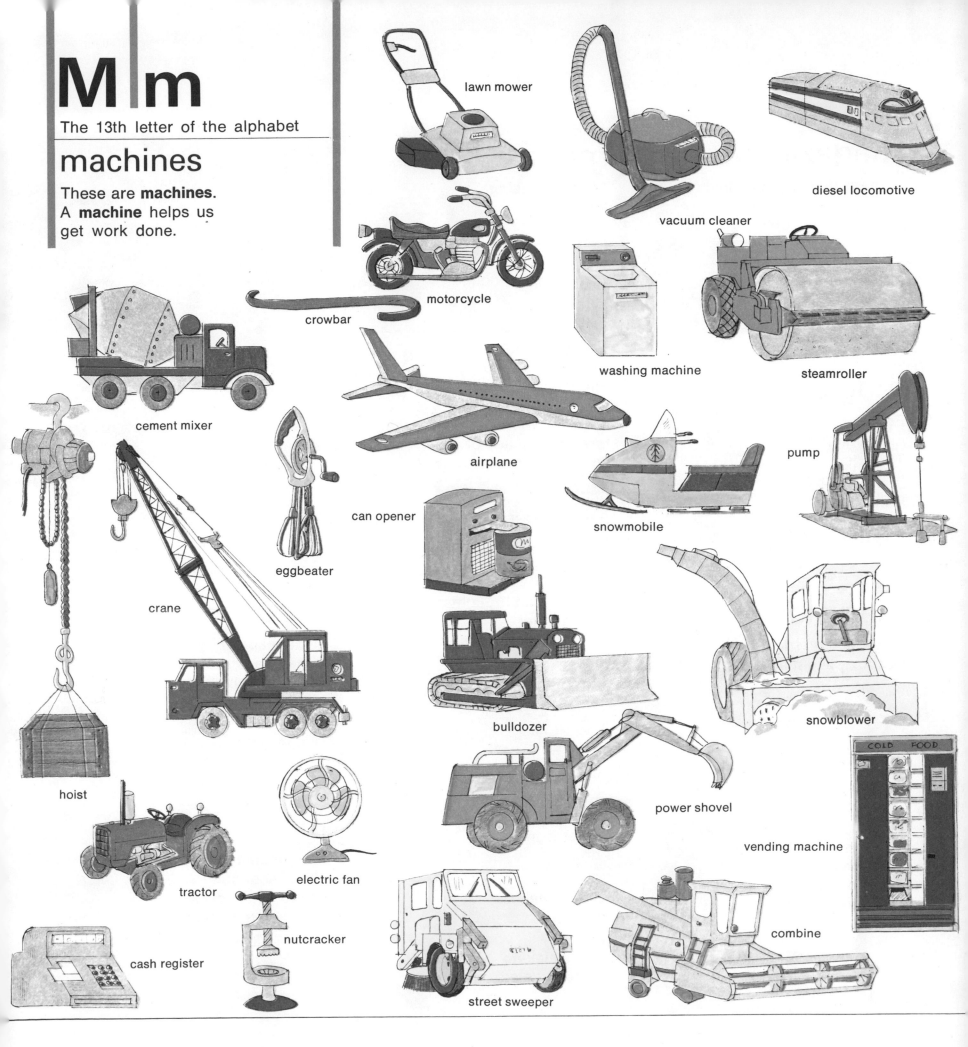

lawn mower

vacuum cleaner

diesel locomotive

motorcycle

crowbar

washing machine

steamroller

cement mixer

airplane

pump

can opener

snowmobile

eggbeater

crane

bulldozer

snowblower

power shovel

hoist

vending machine

tractor

electric fan

combine

nutcracker

cash register

street sweeper

magazine

A **magazine** is something like a book.
Does the mailman bring any **magazines** to your house?

magic

Fairies in stories do **magic**.
They do things that cannot really happen.

magician

Magicians do tricks that look like magic.

magnet

Val is using a **magnet.**
Magnets pick up things with iron in them.
Magnets are not all the same shape.

mail (mails / mailed / mailing)

Cindy is **mailing** a letter.
The **mail** in the mailbox will go to different people.

mailbox

The mailman puts letters sent to you in your own **mailbox.**
Is yours like any of these **mailboxes?**

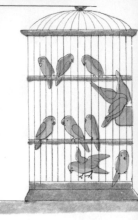

mailman (mailmen)

The **mailman** brought Tess a letter.
He has many letters in his cart.
He has packages and magazines in it too.

make (makes / made / making)

Mother is **making** a dress.

Julie is **making** her bed.

Jake is **making** too much noise.

man (men)

Denny will be a **man** when he grows up.
Fathers are **men.**
These **men** are at a ball game.

many

There are **many** birds in the cage.
How **many** birds are at the feeder?

map

Road **maps** are good to have on car trips.
They show how to get to different places.

maple

A big **maple** tree gives lots of shade.
Maple sugar comes from sugar **maples.**

marbles

Marbles is a game.
You play it
with **marbles**.

march (marches / marched / marching)

It is fun to **march**
to music.
Everyone starts **marching**
with his left foot.

March

March is a month.
Some years Easter
comes in **March.**

marigold

A **marigold** is a flower.
It is easy to grow
marigolds.
Marigolds got the "gold"
in their name
from their color.

mark (marks / marked / marking)

Cal **marked** where
the race will start.
"On your **mark,** get set,
go!" he calls.

These are **marks**
we use in writing.
Hunt for them
on this page.

market

A **market** is a place
to buy things.
Some big **markets**
are called
supermarkets.

mask

No one can see who
you are if you wear
a **mask.**
Would you like any
of these **masks**
for Halloween?

match (matches / matched / matching)

Emmy's ribbons
match her socks.
They are
the same color.

match

Daddy is using a **match**
to start a fire
in the camp stove.

matter

Something is
the **matter** with the car.

May

May is a month.
May comes
after April.

maybe

We say **maybe**
when we can't be sure.
Maybe it will rain.

mean (means / meant / meaning)

A word **means** something.
It tells something.

Beth **meant** to take
her lunch.
She planned to take
her lunch.

n o p q r s t u v w x y z

measure (measures / measured / measuring)

The boys are **measuring**
each other.
They want to know
how tall they are.

Mother **measured**
out a cup of sugar.

meat

Meat is good food.
These **meats** come
from farm animals.

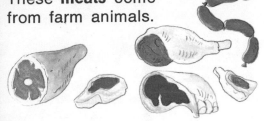

medicine

Sometimes we take
medicine to help us
get well or to help
us stay well.

meet (meets / met / meeting)

Seth is running
to **meet** his grandmother.

The boys' band
met yesterday.

melt (melts / melted / melting)

When snow and ice **melt,**
they change to water.

Lila's chocolate candy
is **melting** in her hand.

mend (mends / mended / mending)

Jay's pants need
to be **mended.**
They need a patch.

The men are **mending**
holes in the street.

merry-go-round

The children are on
the **merry-go-round.**
They go up and down
and around and around.
What animal
on the **merry-go-round**
do you like to ride on?

mess

Curt's room is a **mess.**
It needs cleaning up.

metal

There are many **metals.**
Pennies, nickels,
dimes, and quarters
are made of **metal.**
Do you have
any **metal** toys?

middle

The **middle** button is red.

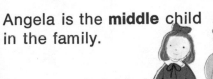

Angela is the **middle** child
in the family.

The paper is folded
in the **middle.**

mile

A **mile** tells how far.
A **mile** is a long way
to walk.
Jet planes fly hundreds
of **miles** in an hour.

milk

Milk comes from cows.
Children need to drink
milk every day.

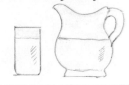

a b c d e f g h i j k l **m**

mill

Grain is made into flour
in a flour **mill.**
Cotton **mills** make
thread and cloth.
Steel **mills** make steel.
Paper **mills** make paper.

mind (minds / minded / minding)

Pal **minds** Bobby.
He does
what Bobby
tells him to.

Do you **mind** waiting?
Do you care
if you have to wait?
We think
and remember
with our **minds.**

minute

A **minute** is 60 seconds long.
There are 60 **minutes** in an hour.

mirror

You can see yourself
in a **mirror.**
Mirrors are made
of glass.

miss (misses / missed / missing)

Meg **missed** the bus.

If Ed **misses** the nail,
he may hit his thumb.

When Mother is away,
the children **miss** her.

mistake

Everybody makes
a **mistake** now and then.
He does something wrong.
Can you find
four **mistakes** here?

mitten

Mittens are for hands.
A **mitten** has one place
for the fingers and
one for the thumb.

mix (mixes / mixed / mixing)

Mother is **mixing** peas
and carrots.

The socks are all
mixed up.

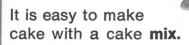

It is easy to make
cake with a cake **mix.**

Monday

Monday is a day of the week.
Monday comes after Sunday.

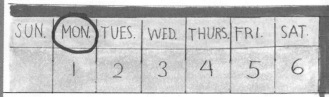

money

Money is used
to buy things.
Rachel has the **money**
for an ice cream cone.

monkey

A **monkey** has
long arms and a tail.
Some **monkeys** can swing
by their tails.

month

It takes twelve **months**
to make a year.
In what **month**
does your birthday
come?

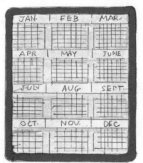

n o p q r s t u v w x y z

moon

On many nights you can see the **moon** in the sky. Does it always look the same? The astronauts are on the **moon**.

moonlight

Moonlight is not as bright as sunshine. It is brightest when the moon looks big and round.

mop (mops / mopped / mopping)

Doug **mopped** up the mud he brought in.

Mops are for cleaning floors.

more

Al wants **more** cake. He wants another piece. The **more** he eats, the **more** he wants.

morning

The sun comes up in the **morning.**
Morning lasts till noon.
Mother said,
"Good **morning**, Jennifer. It's time to get up."

morning glory

A **morning glory** is a flower.
Morning glories close in the afternoon.

mosquito

A **mosquito** is a tiny insect.

Mosquitoes bite.

most

Al ate the **most** cake.
Most people like cake.

motel

A **motel** is a hotel. There are places for cars at **motels**.

moth

A **moth** is an insect. **Moths** are very much like butterflies. Most **moths** fly at night. Have you ever seen **moths** like these?

luna moth

gypsy moth

cecropia moth

mother

Here is Bill's **mother**. She is Betty's **mother** too. Bill and Betty are her children. They call her Mommy.

mountain

A **mountain** is bigger and higher than a hill. There is always snow on some **mountains.**

a b c d e f g h i j k l **m**

64

mouse (mice)

A **mouse** is
a small furry animal
with a long, thin tail.
Mice come into houses.

mouth

You use your **mouth**
for eating and talking.

Most animals
have **mouths.**

move (moves / moved / moving)

Roger's family is **moving**
to a new home.

The hands
on Benjy's toy clock
move.

Tabby **moved**
her kittens
to the basket.

movie

Movies are
moving pictures.
Daddy is showing
a **movie** he took
of the children playing.

much

How **much** candy is left?
The bump didn't hurt **much.**

mud

Mud is soft, wet earth.
The children are making **mud** pies.

museum

You can see many things
in a **museum.**
Here are some things
to see
in different **museums.**

music

Music is made up
of sounds we like to hear.
We sing and dance
to some **music.**
We march to some.
Some we just listen to.

nail

You have **nails**
on your fingers and toes.
Nails like these
hold things together.
They are made of metal.

name (names / named / naming)

Bob **named** his dog Pal.
The children have cards
that tell their **names.**
Is your **name** the same
as one of theirs?

nap

Eddie is taking a **nap.**
The kitten is asleep
too.

napkin

Becky had a **napkin**
in her lunch box.
She is using it
to wipe her fingers.

n o p q r s t u v w x y z

narrow

The door is **narrow.**
It is not wide.

near

Benjy likes to sit **near** the window.
He likes to sit by the window.

neck

A turkey has a long **neck.**

What do Joy and Tina have around their **necks?**

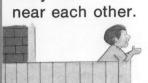

need (needs / needed / needing)

Denny **needs** new shoes.

Rags **needed** a bath.

needle

A **needle** is for sewing.
There are **needles** for knitting too.

neighbor

Ralph and Randy are **neighbors.**
They live near each other.

nest

Many animals build **nests.**
Have you ever seen a squirrel's **nest**

or a robin's **nest**

or an ant **nest?**

new

Lucia's dress is **new.**
She has not had it long.

Carl has a **new** bicycle.
Isn't it shiny?

news

Daddy is listening to the **news.**
He is finding out what is happening.

newspaper

A **newspaper** tells the news.

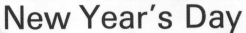

New Year's Day

New Year's Day is the first day of the year.

next

Alice is standing **next** to Donna.
Joel is always asking, "Is it my turn **next**?"

nice

Is today a **nice** day?
Is the weather good?

nickel

A **nickel** is money.
Five pennies make a **nickel.**

a b c d e f g h i j k l m

night

Night comes after the sun goes down. It gets dark at **night**.

nine

Nine tells how many.

9

Nine children are playing a game.

There are **nine** cookies on the plate.

no

Can you put a broken egg together again? The answer is **no**.

There is **no** green thread.

nobody

The chair is empty. **Nobody** is in it.

There is **nobody** at home to answer the telephone.

noise

Noises are sounds. An airplane makes a loud **noise**. The children are making a loud **noise** too.

none

None means not any. **None** of the puppies have long tails.

None of the flowers are red.

noon

Noon comes in the middle of the day. At **noon** the clock says 12.

north

Dick is pointing **north**. He is pointing to the **North** Star.

nose

You use your **nose** for smelling. You use your **nose** for breathing too. Many animals have **noses**.

note

Mother has left a **note** for Ricky. A **note** is a short letter.

RICKY, DON'T FORGET YOUR LUNCH. MOM

nothing

Nothing means not anything. The sack was full of peanuts. Now there is **nothing** in it. The peanuts are all gone.

November

November is a month. Thanksgiving comes in **November**.

n o p q r s t u v w x y z

now

Spot wants his dinner **now**.
He wants it this minute.

number

Two is a small **number**.
Name a bigger **number**.

2

This is Henry's telephone **number**.
Do you know yours?

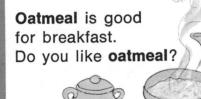

nurse

Nurses take care of sick people.
Joan and Maria are playing **nurse**.

nut

A **nut** has a shell.
Point to the **nuts** you like.

walnut
almond
filbert
Brazil nut
peanut

O|o

The 15th letter of the alphabet

oak

Oak trees are strong.
They live a long time.
There are many kinds.
The seeds of **oaks** are in acorns.

oatmeal

Oatmeal is good for breakfast.
Do you like **oatmeal**?

ocean

The **ocean** is the sea.
Its water is deep.
There is still much to find out about the **ocean**.

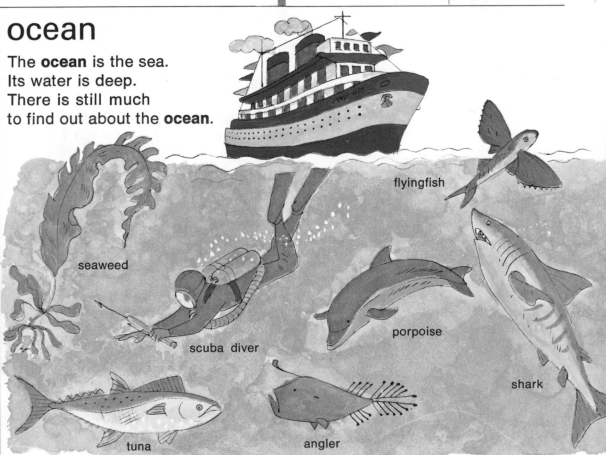

flyingfish
seaweed
scuba diver
porpoise
shark
tuna
angler

o'clock

Carl gets up at seven **o'clock**.
The hands of the clock are like this.

At eight **o'clock** the hands are like this.

October

October is a month.
Halloween comes in **October**.

October
SUN	MON	TUES	WED	THUS	FRI	SAT
		1	2	3	4	5
6	7	8	9	10	11	12
13	14	15	16	17	18	19
20	21	22	23	24	25	26
27	28	29	30	31		

a b c d e f g h i j k l m

of

The store is full **of** things to buy.

The crown is made **of** paper.

off

Lucia is taking **off** Spot's collar.

The wind is blowing leaves **off** the tree.

office

The men are working in an **office**.
Many people work in **offices**.

often

Do you **often** go to the zoo?
Tommy **often** wonders what to play.

oil

The man is putting **oil** in the car.
Oil helps a car run.
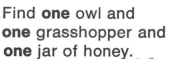

old

The automobile is **old**.
It was made long ago.

The man is **old**.
He has lived many years.

How **old** are you?

on

The robin is **on** the fence.
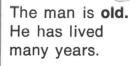

Greg's boots are **on** his feet.

once

Once means one time.
Chris caught a big fish **once**.
Once Debby took a trip in an airplane.
She wants to go **again**.

one

One tells how many.

Find **one** owl and **one** grasshopper and **one** jar of honey.

onion

An **onion** is a vegetable.
We eat **onions** raw or cooked.

only

Only one of the little kittens is black.

There are **only** two pieces of candy left in the sack.

open (opens / opened / opening)

Marcia is **opening** a box.
Jane **opened** hers first.

The door is **open**.

orange

Oranges are sweet and juicy.

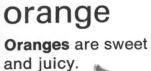

Orange is a color.
Oranges are **orange**.

orchard

A peach **orchard** has many peach trees in it.
A cherry **orchard** has many cherry trees in it.
What kind of **orchard** is this?

organ

Organs make music.
This is a big church **organ**.

ostrich

An **ostrich** is a big bird.
Ostriches cannot fly, but they can run fast.

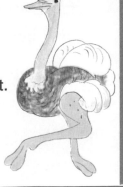

other

One dog is tall.
The **other** is short.

One kite is red.
What color is the **other** one?

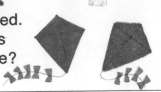

outdoors

Roger is going **outdoors** to play.
Silky is **outdoors** now.

outside

A walnut has a hard shell on the **outside**.

The **outside** of Bill's jacket is red.

Why is the monkey reaching **outside** its cage?

oven

A pie is baking in the **oven**.

over

Joe is climbing **over** the fence to get the ball.
He will throw it **over** to Archie.

Joe is **over** his cold.

overalls

Overalls are work clothes.
Doug's **overalls** are just like Daddy's

owl

An **owl** is a bird.
Owls hunt for food after dark.
Owls have big eyes.

own

Kathy has her **own** toothbrush and her **own** comb.
They belong to her.

a b c d e f g h i j k l m

P p

The 16th letter of the alphabet

pack (packs / packed / packing)

Daddy is **packing**
a bag.
He is putting
his clothes in a bag.

The bus is **packed.**
It is full of people.

package

Connie's new jacket
is in one
of the **packages.**
Which **package** is it?

page

You are looking at a **page**
in your dictionary.
All books have **pages.**

pail

Pails and buckets are
alike.
David's **pail** is empty.
What do you think is
in Stan's **pail**?

paint (paints / painted / painting)

George is **painting**
his wagon red.

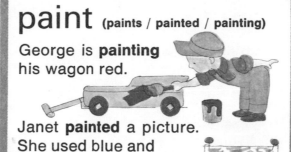

Janet **painted** a picture.
She used blue and
green and yellow **paint.**

pair

Two things that belong
together are a **pair.**
Here are a **pair**
of mittens and a **pair**
of birds.

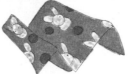

palm

The **palm** of your hand
is the inside part.

A **palm** is a tree.
Palms have
all their leaves
at the top.

pan

There is a **pan**
on the stove.
We use **pans** for cooking.

paper

Paper is good to draw on
and write on and
wrap packages with.
The pages of this book
are made of **paper.**

parachute

His **parachute** keeps
a sky diver
from falling too fast.

parade

Here comes the **parade!**
Parades are fun
for everyone to watch.

park (parks / parked / parking)

Daddy is **parking**
the car in a garage.

Toby and Zeke
are playing in the **park.**

n o p q r s t u v w x y z

parking lot

A shopping center has a big **parking lot.** **Parking lots** are outdoors.

part

Nora ate **part** of the apple. She didn't eat it all.

Here are the **parts** of a toy airport.

Clare has a **part** in her hair.

party

Edith is having a **party.** She invited five friends.

pass (passes / passed / passing)

Judy said, "Please **pass** the jelly."

The red car is **passing** the blue one.

past

It is half **past** two. It is half an hour after two o'clock.

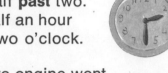

The fire engine went **past** Ben's house. It went by Ben's house.

paste (pastes / pasted / pasting)

Peg is **pasting** pictures on a big piece of paper. She uses **paste** to make them stick.

pat (pats / patted / patting)

Don is **patting** the colt.

Daddy gave Willie a **pat** on the back.

patch

The jacket has leather **patches** on the elbows.

Sometimes a **patch** covers up a hole.

paw

The puppy put a **paw** on Fred's knee.

The cat is licking one of her **paws.**

pay (pays / paid / paying)

Daddy **paid** for the ice cream cones. He gave the man money for them.

pea

A **pea** is a vegetable.

We cook **peas** before we eat them.

peach

A **peach** is a fruit. **Peaches** grow on trees.

a b c d e f g h i j k l m

peanut

A **peanut** shell is easy to open.

Peanut butter is made from **peanuts.**

Do you like **peanut** butter sandwiches?

pear

A **pear** is a fruit. **Pears** grow on trees.

pebble

A **pebble** is a small, smooth stone. Some **pebbles** are pretty.

peek (peeks / peeked / peeking)

Nicky is **peeking** around the corner.

pen

A **pen** is for writing with ink.

pen

The rabbits and the guinea pigs are in **pens.**

pencil

Pencils are to write with.
You can draw pictures with a **pencil** too.

penny

Cal is putting a **penny** in his bank.
He has four more **pennies** to put in.

people

Look at all the **people!**
Men and women and boys and girls are **people.**

pets

Each of these animals is someone's **pet.**
Do you have any **pets?**

canary

toad

burro

gerbil

chameleon

guinea pig

goldfish

kitten

mouse

parakeet

parrot

puppy

rabbit

turtle

n o **p** q r s t u v w x y z

piano

A **piano** makes music.
Karen is playing
the **piano.**

Judy has a toy **piano.**

pick (picks / picked / picking)

Ginnie is **picking**
dandelions.
She has **picked** three.
Ron is **picking** out a car.
Which one would you **pick?**

Buddy dropped his book.
What will he do now?

pickle

A **pickle** is good
to eat with a sandwich.
Some **pickles** are sour.
Some are sweet.

picnic

This family is having
a **picnic.**
At **picnics** we eat
outdoors.

picture

These **pictures** are
in Ann's home.
Find the **picture**
of Ann.

pie

This is an apple **pie.**
What kind of **pie**
do you like best?

piece

Linda is eating
a **piece** of pie.

The cup broke
in **pieces.**

pig

A **pig** is a farm animal.
Pigs are raised
for meat.

pigeon

A **pigeon** is a bird.
We often see **pigeons**
in cities.
These **pigeons** are
finding peanuts to eat.

pile (piles / piled / piling)

Peter is **piling** up
leaves.

Penny is putting the
towels in a **pile.**

pillow

Do you sleep with
your head on a **pillow?**

Pillows are soft.

pilot

The **pilot** of an airplane
flies the plane.
Ships have **pilots**
to sail them.

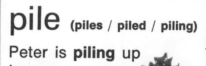

a b c d e f g h i j k l m

pin (pins / pinned / pinning)

Doris **pinned**
her doll's dress together.
She used a big **pin.**

Mother uses **pins**
when she sews.

pine

A **pine** tree is green
the year around.
Some Christmas trees
are **pines.**

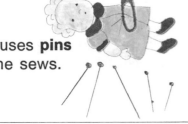

pineapple

A **pineapple** is a fruit.
Pineapples are not
apples and they do not
grow on pines.

pint

A **pint** tells how much.
Here are a **pint**
of ice cream and
a **pint** of cream and
two **pints** of paint.

pitcher

A **pitcher** holds things
like milk and cream
and orange juice.
It is easy to pour
from **pitchers.**

pizza

A **pizza** looks something
like a pie.

place

Tad and his big sister
went many **places** today.
They went to the zoo
and to the playground
and to some stores.

Then they came home.
"Home is the best **place**,"
Tad said.

plan (plans / planned / planning)

Liz is **planning** a party.
She is thinking
what children to invite
and what games to play
and what to have to eat.
She is making a **plan.**

plant (plants / planted / planting)

Rob and his father
are **planting** a maple tree.
The petunias grew
from seeds Rob **planted**.
There are many kinds
of **plants**.
Some **plants** grow wild.

petunia

Balsam fir

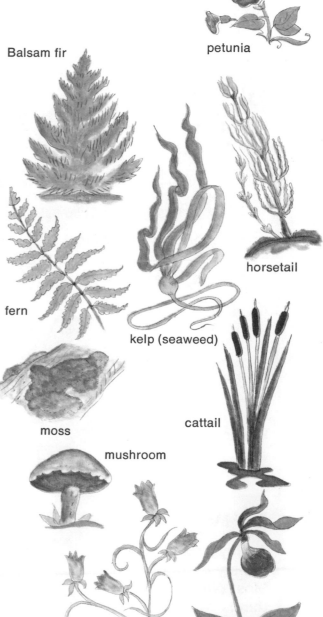

horsetail

fern

kelp (seaweed)

moss

mushroom

cattail

bellflower

moccasin flower

plastic

Many things we use are made of **plastic.** The toy animals are **plastic**.

So is the bag.

So are the knives and forks and spoons.
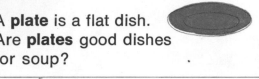

plate

A **plate** is a flat dish. Are **plates** good dishes for soup?
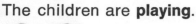

play (plays / played / playing)

The children are **playing**.

Doug **plays** the violin.

Ed and Will are a horse in a **play**. Ed is the front part. Will is the back part.

playground

A **playground** is a place to play outdoors. Most **playgrounds** have things to play on.
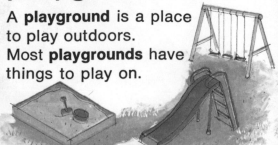

please (pleases / pleased / pleasing)

Sometimes Billy forgets to say **please**. "Say **please**, Billy," Mother says.

plenty

Nan has **plenty** of paper to wrap the package.

Earl has on **plenty** of clothes to keep him warm.

plow (plows / plowed / plowing)

A farmer **plows** a field before he plants seeds in it.

He uses a **plow**. Another kind of **plow** clears away snow.

pocket

Denny has his hands in his **pockets**.

Eloise's dress has a big **pocket**.

point (points / pointed / pointing)

The boys are **pointing** to the things they want to buy.

Pencils and pins and nails have **points**.

poke (pokes / poked / poking)

Andy is **poking** a stick in the mud.
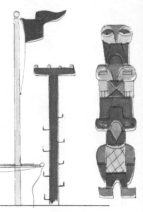

pole

A **pole** is long and not very big around. One of these **poles** is holding up a flag.

policeman (policemen)

The **policeman** is telling the cars to stop. Can you guess why? **Policemen** help keep everybody safe.

a b c d e f g h i j k l m

polite

It is **polite** to say "please"
when you ask for something
and "thank you" when you get it.
It is not **polite** to talk
when someone else is talking.

pond

A **pond** is
a little lake.
What lives in this **pond**?

pony

A **pony** is a small horse.
Ponies are the right size
for children to ride.

pop (pops / popped / popping)

Sara blew too much air
into her balloon.
It **popped**.
A **pop** is not
a very loud noise.

popcorn

Did you ever hear
popcorn popping?

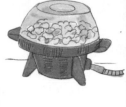

post

One **post** holds a sign.

Another **post** has
a light on top.

Fence **posts** keep fences
from falling down.

potato (potatoes)

A **potato** is a vegetable.
Do you like
baked **potatoes**?

pound

A **pound** tells how heavy.
Here are a **pound**
of butter and a **pound**
of sugar and ten **pounds**
of potatoes.
How many **pounds**
do you weigh?

pound (pounds / pounded / pounding)

Bud is **pounding**
a post into the ground.
He has to hit it hard.

pour (pours / poured / pouring)

Amy is **pouring**
orange juice into a glass.

Outdoors the rain
is **pouring** down.

present

Uncle Bill is giving
Alice a **present**.
What do you think
the **present** is?

pretend (pretends / pretended / pretending)

Martha **pretends**
her doll is a real baby.

Norman is **pretending**
to be a policeman.

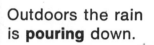

n o **p** q r s t u v w x y z

pretty

Pretty things are good to see or hear.

Eloise wore a **pretty** dress and sang a **pretty** song.

prince

A son of a king and queen is a **prince**.

princess

A daughter of a king and queen is a **princess**.

print (prints / printed / printing)

John is learning to **print** his name. The words in books are **printed** by machines.

prize

Kim won a **prize** for having the quietest pet at the pet show.

promise (promises / promised / promising)

Marty **promised** to stay out of the street. Mother knows he will keep his **promise**.

pudding

Pudding is soft and tastes sweet. Do you like **pudding**?

puddle

A **puddle** of water is not very deep.

puff (puffs / puffed / puffing)

In the story the wolf **puffed** and **puffed** and blew the house down.

Larry blew out the candles with one **puff**.

pull (pulls / pulled / pulling)

The baby is **pulling** his sister's hair.

Arthur **pulls** his **pull** toy across the floor.

pumpkin

A **pumpkin** grows on a vine. **Pumpkins** are used to make **pumpkin** pie. What do we make for Halloween from **pumpkins**?

punch (punches / punched / punching)

June **punched** a hole in the sack.

Leo is **punching** his **punching** bag.

puppet

A **puppet** is a doll made to be moved. We move some **puppets** with our fingers. We move some by pulling strings.

a b c d e f g h i j k l m

puppy

A **puppy** is a baby dog.
Puppies play a lot.

push (pushes / pushed / pushing)

Fran is **pushing**
a wheelbarrow.

Pam said, "**Push** me
higher!"
Perry gave Pam
a big **push**.

put (puts / put / putting)

Angela **put** supper on the table.
Louis **put** on his shoes.
The children **put** on a show.
The firemen **put** out the fire.

puzzle

Kathy is doing a **puzzle**.
She is putting
the pieces together
to make a picture.
What will the picture be?

Q q

The 17th letter of the alphabet

quack (quacks / quacked / quacking)

Ducks **quack**.
A duck's **quack**
may be loud.

quail

A **quail** is a bird.
Baby **quails** look like
baby chickens.

quart

A **quart** tells how much.
Here are a **quart**
of oil and
two **quarts** of milk.

quarter

A **quarter** is money.
Four **quarters** make
a dollar.

queen

A king's wife
is a **queen**.
Some rulers
are **queens**.

question

"How deep is the sea?"
This is a **question**.
Children ask many **questions**.
Do you?

quick

Mary is **quick**.
She will catch
the vase her kitten
knocked over.

quiet

Everybody in the house
has gone to bed.
It is **quiet**.
Not even the mouse
is making a noise.

quite

Harry is not
quite ready to go
to school.
What is he looking for?

n o p **q** r s t u v w x y z

R r

The 18th letter of the alphabet

rabbit

A **rabbit** is a small animal with soft fur.
Rabbits have big ears.

race

The boys are running a **race**.

There are **race** tracks for horse **races** and automobile **races** and dog **races**.

radio

A **radio** brings us news and music.
Many cars have **radios**.

radish

A **radish** is a vegetable.
Radishes are good raw.

rag

Lucy's mother made her a **rag** doll.

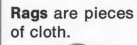

Rags are pieces of cloth.

rain (rains / rained / raining)

It is **raining** too hard to play outdoors.
Rain is made of drops of water.
It falls from clouds.

rainbow

After a rain, there may be a **rainbow** in the sky.
Have you ever seen two **rainbows** at the same time?

raincoat

Raincoats keep us from getting wet in the rain.

raise (raises / raised / raising)

Jerry is **raising** the flag.

Tom **raises** vegetables in his garden.

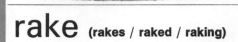

rake (rakes / raked / raking)

The children are **raking** leaves.
Peter has a big **rake**.

rat

A **rat** has a sharp nose and a long tail.
Rats look like big mice.

rattle

A **rattle** is a toy for a baby.

raw

Raw food is food that is not cooked.

a b c d e f g h i j k l m

reach (reaches / reached / reaching)

The cat is up too high for Daddy to **reach**.

read (reads / read / reading)

Sara is **reading** a book.

Sam **read** it yesterday.

ready

This family is **ready** to go on a trip. Everybody has the things he will need.

real

Which is the **real** bear?

record

We can buy **records** of music we like. A **record** is played on a machine.

red

Red is a color.

Here are a **red** rose

and a **red** heart and

a big **red** barn.

refrigerator

A **refrigerator** keeps food cold.

reindeer

Reindeer live where it is very cold in winter. Do you know the song about a red-nosed **reindeer**?

remember

(remembers / remembered / remembering)

Amy **remembered** Joy's birthday. She did not forget it. Do you **remember** what you ate for lunch yesterday?

rest (rests / rested / resting)

When we get tired, we need to **rest**. Grandfather often **rests** his eyes.

The cowboy is **resting** his horse.

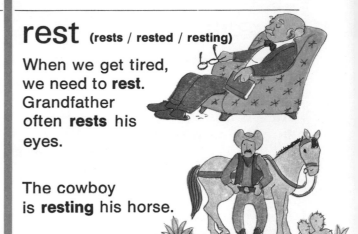

rest

Cathy had a dollar. She bought a paper doll with some of it. She saved the **rest**.

restaurant

Molly's family is eating in a **restaurant**.

ribbon

Sue has a pink **ribbon** in her hair.

Ribbons make packages look pretty.

rice

Rice is a grain.
It is good with meat
and vegetables.
Rice is good
in pudding too.

riddle

Here is a **riddle**.
"What goes up and down
at the same time?"
One picture tells
the answer.

ride (rides / rode / ridden / riding)

Jay **rides** a bicycle.
Pepper is **riding**
in the basket.
Mark is having a **ride**
in a boat.

right

Mary is waving
her **right** hand.

The owl's **right** eye
is shut.

Do you know
the **right** answer
to the riddle?

ring (rings / rang / rung / ringing)

Sally is **ringing** a bell.

The telephone **rang**
a long time.

Connie has a new **ring**.

Stan drew a **ring**
around the kangaroo.

ripe

The apple is **ripe**.
It is sweet and ready
to eat.

river

The water in a **river**
runs down to the sea.
Some **rivers** are
deep enough
for big boats.

road

The **road** is
wide enough for many cars.
Some **roads** are only
wide enough for one.

robin

A **robin** is a bird.
Do you know a **robin**
when you see one?

rock

The mountain is made
of **rock**.
This **rock**
was brought back
from the moon.

rock (rocks / rocked / rocking)

Judy is **rocking**
her doll.

rocket

The big **rocket**
is going up.
Tony's **rocket** is a toy.

rodeo

A **rodeo** is
a cowboy show.

a b c d e f g h i j k l m

roll (rolls / rolled / rolling)

The little cars are **rolling** down the board.

The man **rolled** up the rug.

Rolls are like bread.

Paper towels come in **rolls.**

roller skates

Roller skates have wheels that roll.

roof

A **roof** covers the top of a building.

room

A house or apartment may have only one **room**. It may have many **rooms**.

Is there **room** in the car for everybody?

rooster

Some grown-up chickens are **roosters**.
Did a **rooster** ever wake you up with his "cock-a-doodle-doo?"

root

The **roots** of the tree are in the ground. They take in water for the tree.

A radish is the **root** of a radish plant.

rope

The cowboy is using a **rope** to catch a calf.

Sailors use **ropes.**

rose

A **rose** is a flower.
Are all **roses** the same color?

rough

The road is **rough**. It is not smooth.

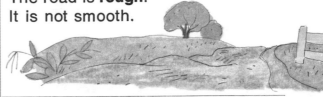

round

The ball is **round.**

So is the hoop.

A telephone pole is **round** too.

row

The children are standing in a **row**. They are in front of a **row** of flags.

row (rows / rowed / rowing)

Jimmy helps his father **row** the boat.
Rowing it makes it go.

rub (rubs / rubbed / rubbing)

Ed is **rubbing** his shoes to make them shine.

rubber

All these things are made of **rubber**.

rug

Rugs are for floors. Blackie is asleep in the middle of the **rug**.

ruler

Countries have **rulers**. A **ruler** leads his country.

A **ruler** helps us measure.

run (runs / ran / run / running)

The boy and the dog and the pony are **running**. Do you **run** when you are in a hurry?

The river **runs** over the edge and falls.

S s

The 19th letter of the alphabet

sack

A **sack** is a bag.

Daddy bought two **sacks** of potatoes.

Ray won the **sack** race.

safe

Rudy was lost. Now he is **safe** at home.

Is the bird in a **safe** place?

sail (sails / sailed / sailing)

The boat is **sailing** across the lake. The **sails** are catching the wind.

salt

Salt makes some foods taste better.

same

These boys have the **same** name. They are both named George. Rita wore the **same** dress last Monday.

sand

Sand comes from rock. In some places there are big hills of **sand**.

sandwich

Bread and jelly and peanut butter make one kind of **sandwich**. What do you like in **sandwiches**?

Saturday

Saturday is the last day of the week. **Saturday** comes after Friday.

a b c d e f g h i j k l m

saucer

Here are three **saucers**.
Find a cup for each **saucer**.

save (saves / saved / saving)

Gus **saves** bottle caps.
Gus keeps bottle caps.

saw

A **saw** is a tool
for cutting hard things
like wood and metal.
Saws have sharp teeth.

say (says / said / saying)

The baby can **say** three words.
Mother **said**, "The baby
is learning to talk."

scale

A **scale** tells how much
something weighs.

Which **scale** is the one
for weighing you?

scare (scares / scared / scaring)

Chris is trying
to **scare** Dolores.
Would you be **scared**?

school

We go to **school** when
we are old enough.
Some of the things
we learn in **schools**
we learn from books.

scissors

Jamie's **scissors** cut
paper.
Mother has big **scissors**
to cut cloth and
tiny ones to cut her nails.

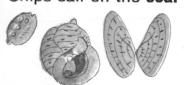

scooter

Rex can go fast
on his **scooter**.
Scooters are fun
to ride.

scratch (scratches / scratched / scratching)

Cats sometimes **scratch**
the furniture.

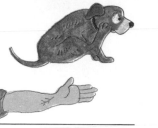

Pal is **scratching**.

Ben got a **scratch**
from a rose bush.

sea

The **sea** is the home
of many animals and plants.
Its water is salty.
Many animals
of the **sea** have shells.
Ships sail on the **sea**.

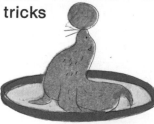

seal

A **seal** has soft fur.
Seals live in the sea.
Many zoos have **seals**.
The **seals** that do tricks
are sea lions.

seat

A **seat** is something
to sit on.

n o p q **r s** t u v w x y z

second

John is **second** in line.
He is next
to the head
of the line.

Nancy's dog won
second prize.

A **second** is a tiny part
of a minute.

secret

Bob and John just found a
robin's nest.

They will not tell anyone.
It will be a **secret**.

see (sees / saw / seen / seeing)

We **see** with our eyes.
Many animals have eyes
and can **see**.
Jim **saw** a giraffe at the zoo.

seed

This is a sunflower **seed**.
Many plants grow from **seeds**.

There are **seeds**
in many fruits and vegetables.

sell (sells / sold / selling)

The man with the **hat**
has balloons to **sell**.
He is **selling** one to Sally.

Sally is paying
him a quarter.

send (sends / sent / sending)

Ann always **sends**
her grandmother
a birthday card.

She is putting
the card in the mailbox.
Mother **sent** Ann to the store.
She asked her to go to the store.

September

September is a month.

Is your birthday in **September**?

set

This is a **set** of colored crayons.

This is a **set** of tools.

set (sets / set / setting)

The sun is **setting**.
The sun is going down.

Nancy **set** a bowl of flowers
on the table.
She put a bowl of flowers
on the table.

seven

Seven tells how many.   7

Here are **seven** toads

and **seven** toadstools

and **seven** tiny tadpoles.

sew (Sews / sewed / sewn / sewing)

You need a needle and
thread to **sew** with.

Debby is **sewing**.
She is making a dress
for her doll.

sewing machine

You can sew fast
with a **sewing machine**.

shade

It is cool in the **shade** of the big tree.

shadow

Here are some **shadows.**

Did you ever see your own **shadow**?

shake (shakes / shook / shaken / shaking)

The baby likes to **shake** his rattle.

The men are **shaking** hands.

shape

A marble and a ball are the same **shape.**

These pieces of paper have different **shapes.**

So do these toys.

sharp

The point of a pin is **sharp.**
The knife has a **sharp** edge.

Arthur has **sharp** eyes.
He saw right away where the kitten was hiding.

sheep

Sheep have coats of soft wool.
We get wool from **sheep.**

shelf (shelves)

The green **shelf** is fastened to the wall.

Ricky's red storybook is on the bottom **shelf** of the bookcase.

shell

Many animals have **shells.**

turtle

armadillo

crab

snail

A bird's egg has a **shell.**

shine (shines / shone / shining)

A cat's eyes **shine** in the dark.

The sun **shines** during the day.

ship

A **ship** is a big boat.

There are many kinds of **ships.**

shirt

The boys all have on **shirts.**

Bill's **shirt** is blue.

shoe

Shoes are for feet.

Jimmy has one **shoe** off and one **shoe** on.

n o p q r **s** t u v w x y z

shoot (shoots / shot / shooting)

Adam is **shooting** an arrow.

shopping center

There are many stores in a **shopping center**.

short

Short means not long or not tall.
Point to the things that are **short**.

shoulder

Lift one **shoulder**.
Timmy likes to ride on his father's **shoulders**.

shovel (shovels / shoveled / shoveling)

Hal is **shoveling** snow with a snow **shovel**.
The big **shovel** can do more work than a man.

show (shows / showed / showing)

Lucia is **showing** her new dress to Liz. After supper the girls watched a **show** on TV.

shut (shuts / shut / shutting)

Greg is **shutting** the window. When it is open, the wind blows his papers about. The door **shut** with a bang.

sick

When you are **sick**, you do not feel well. Someone **sick** has come to the hospital.

side

Matt is on Henry's **side** of the bed.

The boys chose **sides** for the ball game.

sidewalk

A **sidewalk** goes along the side of a street. A city has miles of **sidewalks** for people to walk on.

sign

Mother made a **sign** that means "Be quiet."

How many of these **signs** have you seen?

silk

Silk is spun by silkworms. **Silk** cloth is soft and beautiful.

silver

Silver is a metal. These things are **silver**. Can you tell what each one is?

a b c d e f g h i j k l m

sing (sings / sang / sung / singing)

The bird is **singing**.

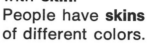

Can you **sing**
the ABC song?
Walt **sang** it
for Abbie
and Tuffy.

sink (sinks / sank / sunk / sinking)

Jan's doll **sank**
to the bottom
of the pool.

Della is washing
her dishes
in the **sink**.

sister

Julie is Joan's **sister**.
They have
the same mother
and father.
Sisters often look
alike.

sit (sits / sat / sitting)

Everybody is **sitting**
down.

The cat **sat**
in the window.

The clock **sits**
on a chest of drawers.

six

Six tells how many.

The bug has **six** legs.

The star has **six** points.

size

Ted is the same **size**
as Tod.
Ted is just as big
as Tod.

Is the hat the right **size**
for Stevie?

skate (skates / skated / skating)

Kate likes to **skate**.
She got new roller **skates**
for her birthday.

ski (skis / skied / skiing)

Keith is **skiing**
in the park.
Skis are made of wood
or metal or plastic.

skin

Your body is covered
with **skin**.
People have **skins**
of different colors.

Peaches have thin **skins**.

skip (skips / skipped / skipping)

Grace **skipped**
all the way to school.

Jack is **skipping** some
of the pages.
He is not reading them.

sky

Some days the **sky**
looks blue.

Some days it is cloudy.

sled

You can slide
on the snow on a **sled**.
Sleds go fast
down the side of a hill.

n o p q r **s** t u v w x y z

sleep (sleeps / slept / sleeping)

Everybody is **sleeping**.
The baby **slept**
all night.
He didn't wake up once.

A chipmunk has
a long winter **sleep**.

slide (slides / slid / sliding)

You can **slide** on ice
without a sled.

The children like
to play on the **slides**
in the park.

slow

Slow means not fast.
Which girl is **slow**?

small

Father bought
a **small** car.
It is not as big
as the old one.

The tricycle is
too **small** for Jake.

smell (smells / smelled / smelling)

Rose is **smelling** a rose.
What **smells** do you like?

smile (smiles / smiled / smiling)

Daddy said **"Smile"** when
he took Lou's picture.
Lou gave a big **smile**.
He looked happy.

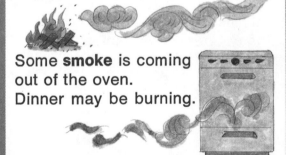

smoke

Smoke comes from fires.

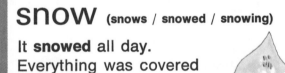

Some **smoke** is coming
out of the oven.
Dinner may be burning.

smooth

A pebble feels **smooth**.

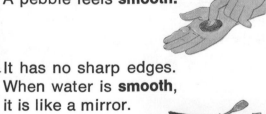

.It has no sharp edges.
When water is **smooth**,
it is like a mirror.

snail

A **snail** has a soft body
and a hard shell.

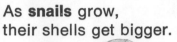

As **snails** grow,
their shells get bigger.

snake

A **snake** is
a long, thin animal
without any legs.
Snakes can crawl
and swim.

snow (snows / snowed / snowing)

It **snowed** all day.
Everything was covered
with **snow.**

snowflake

A **snowflake** is
a tiny bit of snow.
Snowflakes turn
to water when they melt.

a b c d e f g h i j k l m

soap

Soap helps us get things clean. Did you ever get **soap** in your eyes?

socks

Socks are for feet.

soft

These things are **soft**.

Voices and music can be **soft** too.

soldier

Luke's big brother is a **soldier**. **Soldiers** are ready to fight for their country.

somebody

Somebody marked on the wall. Who could it be?

something

Nina has **something** in her hands. What could it be?

son

A boy is the **son** of his mother and father. This mother and father have four **sons**.

song

What **songs** do you like? Can you sing a **song**?

sore

Vic has a **sore** toe. Last week he had a **sore** on one thumb.

sorry

Jamie was **sorry** he made his sister cry. He felt bad about it.

sound

Everything you hear is a **sound**. Think of some **sounds** you heard today.

soup

Soup is made from meat or fish or vegetables. What kind of **soup** do you like best?

sour

These foods are **sour**. They are not sweet.

south

Dick is facing north. His back is to the **south**.

n o p q r **s** t u v w x y z

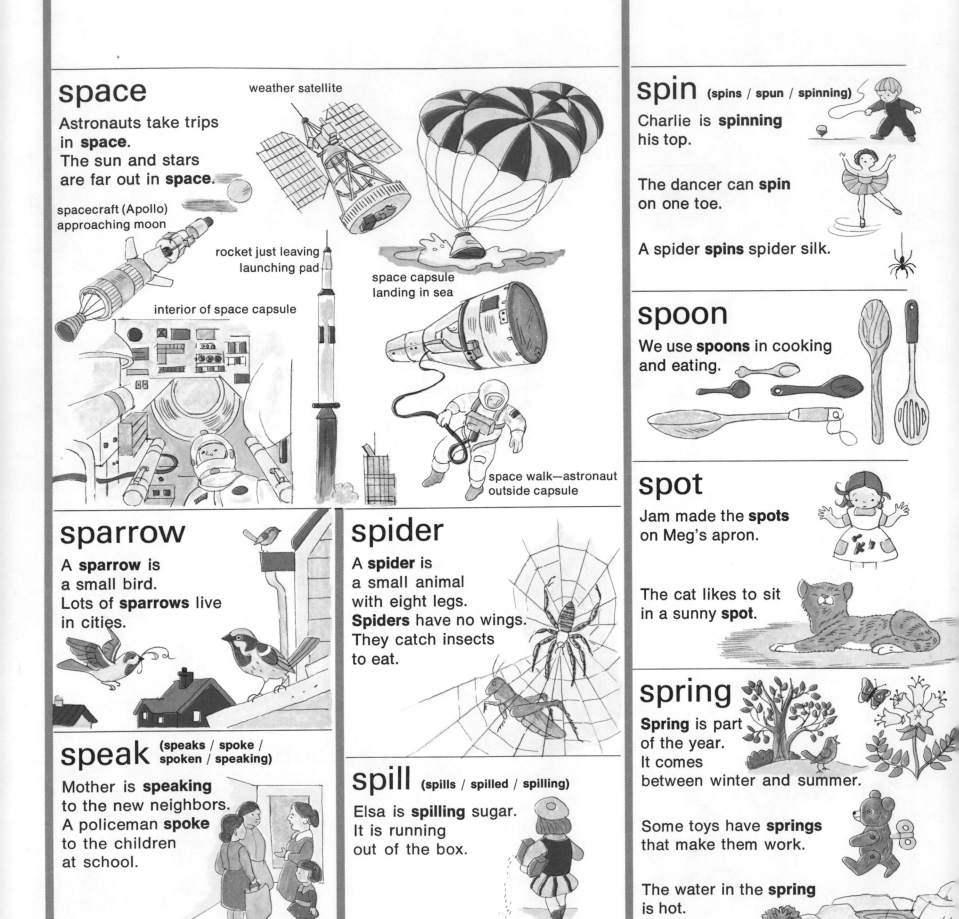

space

Astronauts take trips in **space**.
The sun and stars are far out in **space**.

weather satellite

spacecraft (Apollo) approaching moon

rocket just leaving launching pad

space capsule landing in sea

interior of space capsule

space walk—astronaut outside capsule

sparrow

A **sparrow** is a small bird.
Lots of **sparrows** live in cities.

speak (speaks / spoke / spoken / speaking)

Mother is **speaking** to the new neighbors.
A policeman **spoke** to the children at school.

spider

A **spider** is a small animal with eight legs.
Spiders have no wings. They catch insects to eat.

spill (spills / spilled / spilling)

Elsa is **spilling** sugar.
It is running out of the box.

spin (spins / spun / spinning)

Charlie is **spinning** his top.

The dancer can **spin** on one toe.

A spider **spins** spider silk.

spoon

We use **spoons** in cooking and eating.

spot

Jam made the **spots** on Meg's apron.

The cat likes to sit in a sunny **spot**.

spring

Spring is part of the year.
It comes between winter and summer.

Some toys have **springs** that make them work.

The water in the **spring** is hot.

a b c d e f g h i j k l m

92

square

This is a **square**.
Point to the four corners.

Which piece goes
in the **square** hole?

squeeze (squeezes / squeezed / squeezing)

We **squeeze** an orange
to get its juice.

Seth is **squeezing** out
toothpaste.

Rags **squeezed**
under the fence.

squirrel

A **squirrel** is
a small furry animal
with a big tail.
Squirrels live in trees.

stairs

The **stairs** lead
to the second floor.
Don goes up the **stairs**
two steps at a time.

stamp (stamps / stamped / stamping)

Connie is **stamping**
her foot.

The paper was **stamped**
with a star.

We use **stamps** to send
letters in the mail.

stand (stands / stood / standing)

The bird is **standing**
on one leg.

The children set up
a **stand** to sell lemonade.

star

The flag
has 50 **stars**.

You cannot count
all the **stars**
in the sky at night.

start (starts / started / starting)

The TV show **starts**
at seven o'clock.
Daddy is **starting**
the car.

stay (stays / stayed / staying)

Mother told Ben
to **stay** clean.

Ellen is **staying**
with a friend
for a week.

steel

Steel is a metal.
It is made from iron.
All these things are
steel.

steep

The hill is too **steep**
for coasting.

stem

The **stem** of a plant
grows out of the ground.
When you pick flowers,
you hold them
by the **stems**.

n o p q r **s** t u v w x y z

step (steps / stepped / stepping)

The girls are **stepping** over the puddle.

Bea likes to sit on the bottom **step**.

stick (sticks / stuck / sticking)

Tim **stuck** the hot dog on a **stick**.

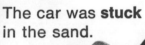

The car was **stuck** in the sand.

The children picked up **sticks** for the fire.

still

You sit **still** to have your picture taken.
You keep **still** when someone else is talking.
Frannie **still** hasn't finished her dinner.

stocking

Sandra's **stockings** match her dress.

stomach

The food you eat goes to your **stomach**.

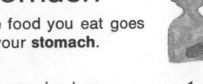

The puppies have full **stomachs**.

stone

A **stone** is a piece of rock.
You can find little **stones** on the ground.

Many buildings are made of **stone**.

stop (stops / stopped / stopping)

The man is **stopping** the cars.

When it **stops** raining, there may be a rainbow.
Daddy **stopped** to buy some bread.

stop sign

This is a **stop sign**.
Cars must stop when they come to **stop signs**.

store

A **store** is a place to buy things.
What **stores** do you like to go to?

storm

In a **storm** the wind blows hard.
It may rain or snow.
There may be thunder and lightning.

story

Annabel is telling the children a **story** about a magic carpet.
She knows lots of good **stories**.

stove

Stoves give heat.
Hamburgers are cooking on top of the **stove**.
What is in the oven?

a b c d e f g h i j k l m

straight

The line is **straight**. ─────
Happy is running **straight** to his dish.

Can you stand up as **straight** as this?

strawberry

A **strawberry** is a fruit.
Strawberries grow on small plants.

street

Towns and cities have **streets**.
This is a busy **street**.

string (strings / strung / stringing)

Patty is **stringing** beads.
She is putting the beads on a **string**.
We buy **string** in balls.

stripe

Here are four things with **stripes**.
Which one has a wide red **stripe**?

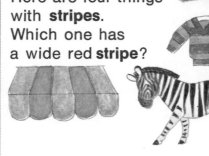

strong

The man is **strong**.
He can lift the heavy weight.

The stick is **strong**.
Leo cannot break it.

submarine

A **submarine** is a boat that can move about under the water.

sugar

Sugar is sweet.
We put **sugar** in other foods to make them taste sweet.

suit

Rob and Ruth have new **suits**.
Rob's **suit** is blue.
Ruth's **suit** is green.

summer

Summer is part of the year.
It comes between spring and fall.

sun

The **sun** warms the earth and gives it light.

Sunday

Sunday is the first day of the week.
Church bells ring on **Sunday** morning.

n o p q r **s** t u v w x y z

sunflower

A **sunflower** is
a yellow flower.
Some **sunflowers** are
very tall.

sunshine

Sunshine is the light
that comes from the sun.

supermarket

A **supermarket** is
a big grocery store.

supper

People eat **supper**
in the evening.
Would this be
a good **supper**?

suppose (supposes / supposed / supposing)

Suppose it is raining.
Pretend it is raining.
Which thing will you
need outdoors?

sure

Mother said, "Are you **sure**
Abe's party is today?
Ask him to make **sure**."

surprise (surprises / surprised / surprising)

The children's present
surprised Mother.
It was a happy **surprise**.
Everybody likes
happy **surprises**.

sweater

A **sweater** is
like a jacket.
It is warm.
Sweaters are made
of yarn.

sweep (sweeps / swept / sweeping)

The big machine
is **sweeping** the street.

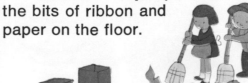

The children **swept** up
the bits of ribbon and
paper on the floor.

sweet

These things are **sweet**.
Which ones do you like?

swim (swims / swam / swimming)

Fish **swim** in the sea.
Vic **swam**
in the **swimming** pool.
He goes for a **swim**
every Saturday.

swimming pool

A **swimming pool** is
a good place to swim.
Some **swimming pools**
are inside buildings.
Some are outdoors.

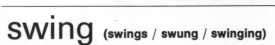

swing (swings / swung / swinging)

The children
are **swinging** high.
Have you ever **swung**
on a **swing**?
The **swings** are
in a playground.

a b c d e f g h i j k l m

T t

The 20th letter of the alphabet

table

A **table** is
a good place for eating
or writing or playing
a game.
What are these **tables** for?

tail

Each of
these animals
has a **tail**.

None of these animals
have **tails**.

Some kites have **tails**.

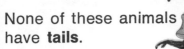

take (takes / took / taking)

"**Take** my hand,"
Joel said to Larry.
"We'll cross together."

Daddy is **taking**
a nap.

talk (talks / talked / talking)

Everybody is **talking**
at the same time.

Jerry has a parrot
that **talks**.

tall

The trees are **tall**.
Their tops are high
above the bushes.
One tree is very **tall**.

tame

This is a
tame animal.
It belongs
to somebody.

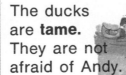

The ducks
are **tame**.
They are not
afraid of Andy.

tank

A **tank** holds lots
of water or gas or oil.
These big **tanks**
are full of oil.

taste (tastes / tasted / tasting)

Sheila is **tasting**
her soup.

Charlie says bananas
taste good.
Do you like the **taste**
of bananas?

taxi

A **taxi** is a car.
We have to pay
to ride in **taxis**.

tea

Tea is a drink
many people like.

telephone

The girls are talking
over the **telephone**.
One of the **telephones**
is red.
What color is
the other one?

television

We hear and watch
television.
Do you call
television TV?

n o p q r **s** t u v w x y z

tell (tells / told / telling)

Penny is **telling** her friends about her trip.

Can you **tell** which bird is a pigeon?

ten

Ten tells how many. **10**

Ten pennies make a dime.
Ten dimes make a dollar.

tent

People often sleep in **tents** when they go camping.
Jack and his father are putting up a **tent**.

thank (thanks / thanked / thanking)

Alex **thanked** Ed for helping him.
He said, "**Thank** you, Ed."

Thanksgiving

Thanksgiving comes in November.
We often eat turkey on **Thanksgiving**.

thermometer

Thermometers tell how hot or how cold.
Which **thermometer** would a doctor use?

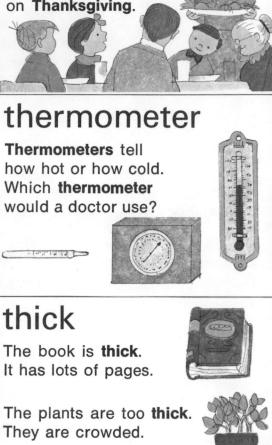

thick

The book is **thick**.
It has lots of pages.

The plants are too **thick**.
They are crowded.

The paint is **thick**.
It is hard to pour.

thin

The book is **thin**.
It has only a few pages.

The man is too **thin**.
He is not fat enough.

The soup is **thin**.
It is easy to pour.

thing

You are sure not to have one of these **things**.
Which **thing** is it?

think (thinks / thought / thinking)

Bruce **thought** he was old enough to ride a bicycle.
His father and mother **thought** so too.
What do you **think**?

thirsty

Benny and his dog are both **thirsty**.
They are glad to have some water to drink.

thread (threads / threaded / threading)

Nora can **thread** a needle.
She is using red **thread**.

a b c d e f g h i j k l m

three

Three tells how many.
Here are **three** boys.
Their hats have
three corners.
Their stools have
three legs.

through

Sharon is peeking
through her fingers.
She is peeking
between her fingers.

Sue is **through**
with her book.
She has read it all.

throw (throws / threw / throwing)

Tony **threw** the ball.
He **throws**
with his right hand.
Do you?

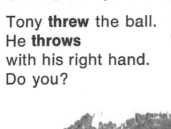

thumb

Your **thumbs**
help you pick up
and hold things.

The **thumb** of the mitten
is red.

thunder

Thunder is a loud noise.
It comes with lightning.
Thunder cannot hurt you.

Thursday

Thursday is a day
of the week.
Thursday comes
after Wednesday.

ticket

Toby and his father
have **tickets**
to the ball game.
They each need
a **ticket** to get in.

tie (ties / tied / tying)

Archie is **tying**
his shoes.
Sometimes he forgets
to **tie** them.

Daddy has a new **tie**.

tiger

A **tiger** is
a big wild animal.
Tigers have stripes.

tight

"Hold on **tight**,"
said Daddy.

Benjy's shoes
are too **tight**.

time

Bert can tell **time**.

The ball bounced
three **times**.
A year is a long **time**.

tiny

The shells are **tiny**.
They are very small.

Which flower is **tiny**?

tip

Jan has paint
on the **tip** of her nose.

tire

The car needs
a new **tire**.

Brad is putting air
in his bicycle **tires**.

tired

The boys are **tired**.
They have been
playing hard.
Do you ever
get **tired?**

to

Barbara is giving
a book
to her mother.
Manuel is
on his way
to the store.
Manuel is good
to his dog Brownie.

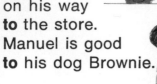

toad

A **toad** is
a small animal.
Toads are like frogs.
They live in water
till they grow up.

toast

A piece of **toast** is
first a piece of bread.
Making the bread very hot
changes it to **toast**.

today

Today is this day.
It was **today** when you got up.
It will still be **today**
when you go to bed.

toe

Buddy's big **toe** shows.
There is a hole in the **toe**
of his sock.

Karen's shoes have
red **toes**.

together

Ned and Gene like
to play **together**.
Together they can
reach around a tree

or look over a wall

or lift a pail of water.

tomato

A **tomato** is a vegetable.
We eat **tomatoes** raw
or cooked.

tomorrow

Tomorrow is the day
after today.
If today is Sunday,
what will **tomorrow** be?

tongue

Your **tongue** helps you
talk.
Say "Little Lulu" and
feel it move.
You taste
with your **tongue** too.

Toads catch insects
with their **tongues**.

tonight

Tonight is the end of today.
It will be **tonight**
when you go to bed.

a b c d e f g h i j k l m

tools

Tools help us work. Do you have any of these **tools** in your house?

ax

drill

pick

hammer

spade

plane

screwdriver

hoe

pliers

chisel

saw

tooth (teeth)

Our **teeth** help us eat. They help us talk too. Mark just lost a **tooth.**

toothbrush

Everybody needs his own **toothbrush**. We use **toothbrushes** to clean our teeth.

top

Tops spin around and around.

top

Steve has a pumpkin on **top** of his head. He wants to look funny.

touch (touches / touched / touching)

The girls' heads are **touching**.

Roy **touched** the frog with his toe.

towel

Towels are for drying things.

town

A **town** is like a city, but it is not as big.

toys

A **toy** is to play with. Do you have any of these **toys**?

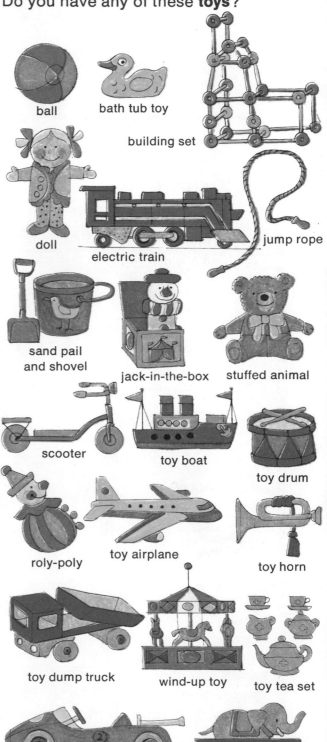

ball

bath tub toy

building set

doll

electric train

jump rope

sand pail and shovel

jack-in-the-box

stuffed animal

scooter

toy boat

toy drum

roly-poly

toy airplane

toy horn

toy dump truck

wind-up toy

toy tea set

toy racing car

pull toy

track

A train runs
on a railroad **track**.

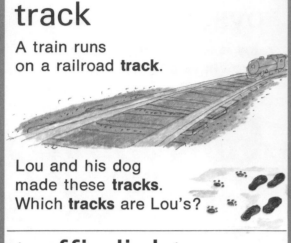

Lou and his dog
made these **tracks**.
Which **tracks** are Lou's?

traffic light

The **traffic light** is red.
It tells you it is not safe
to cross the street.

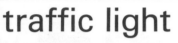

train

The **train** has many cars
to carry things.
A big engine pulls it.

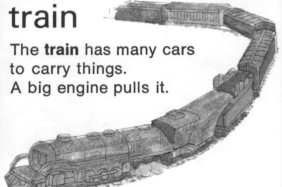

trick

Harry can do **tricks**
with his magic set.

Pal knows a **trick** too.

tricycle

A **tricycle** has
three wheels.
Tricycles are
easy to ride.

trip (trips / tripped / tripping)

Joe **tripped** on the rug.

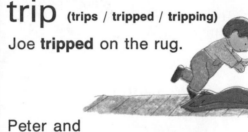

Peter and
the twins like
to go places.
They like
to take **trips**.

truck

A **truck** is a kind
of automobile.
Trucks carry big loads.

true

Fairy stories are not **true**.
True stories tell about things
that really happened.
Oliver told a story
about a ride on a horse
with wings.
Was the story **true**?

trunk

The elephant is using
his **trunk** to get cool.

Trees have **trunks**.

trees

A **tree** is a plant.
No other plants are as big
as the biggest **trees**.
Can you find a **tree**
you know?

cottonwood

magnolia
in bloom

redwood

Royal palm

weeping
willow

live oak

spruce

apple

banyan

a b c d e f g h i j k l m

try (tries / tried / trying)

Tommy is **trying** to catch a butterfly.

Sara is **trying** on a dress.
She has **tried** on three.

Tuesday

Tuesday is a day of the week.
Tuesday comes after Monday.

tulip

A **tulip** is a flower.
We see **tulips** in the spring.

tumble (tumbles / tumbled / tumbling)

The castle is **tumbling** down.

Linda just took a **tumble**.

turkey

A **turkey** is a big bird.
Turkeys are raised for food.

turn (turns / turned / turning)

Walt **turned** the wheel of his car to **turn** the corner.

Nicky is **turning** head over heels.

The boys are taking **turns** diving.

turnip

A **turnip** is a vegetable.
The roots of **turnips** are good to eat.
So are the leaves.

turtle

Turtles are animals with shells.
One **turtle** has shut itself up in its shell.

twelve 12

Twelve tells how many.
Here are **twelve** eggs

and **twelve** doughnuts.

The ladybug has **twelve** spots.

twin

Kim and Kay are **twins**.
They are both five and have the same birthday.
They have the same father and mother.
Do you have a **twin**?

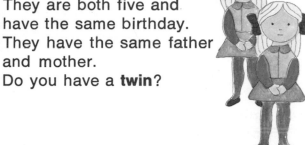

two 2

Two tells how many.

Count **two** bears and

two bees and

two yellow butterflies.

typewriter

A **typewriter** is a machine for writing fast.
Some **typewriters** are electric.

n o p q r s **t** u v w x y z

U u

The 21st letter of the alphabet.

ugly

These animals are **ugly**.
They are not pretty.

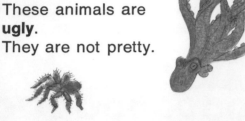

umbrella

An **umbrella**
keeps off
sunshine or rain.

Umbrellas can
be opened
and closed.

uncle

Emily and Jack have two **uncles**.
Uncle Jim is
their mother's brother.
Uncle Bill is
their father's brother.

UNCLE BILL   FATHER   MOTHER   UNCLE JIM

EMILY   JACK

under

The kittens are
under the chair.
Their basket is
under the table.

untie (unties / untied / untying)

David is **untying**
his shoes.

Cathy **untied** the bow
on her present.

up

This is a sign for **up**. ⬆
When Danny goes down,
Harold goes **up**.

The bug crawled
up the leaf.

upstairs

Betty is going **upstairs**.

use (uses / used / using)

Max **used** a carrot
for the snowman's nose.
Lucy **uses**
her dictionary to see
how to write a word.
Grandfather **used**
to have lots of hair.
Now he doesn't.

V v

The 22nd letter of the alphabet

vacation

A **vacation** is a time
away from school
and work.
During **vacations**
we rest and play.
Sometimes we go
on trips.

valentine

Ralph and Mary
are making **valentines**.
They will send them
to their friends
on **Valentine's** Day.

valley

The hotel is at the bottom
of a **valley**.

vase

The blue **vase** has
flowers in it.
Some **vases** are
very pretty.

a b c d e f g h i j k l m

vegetable

A **vegetable** comes from a plant. We eat many kinds of **vegetables**. Pick out the ones you know.

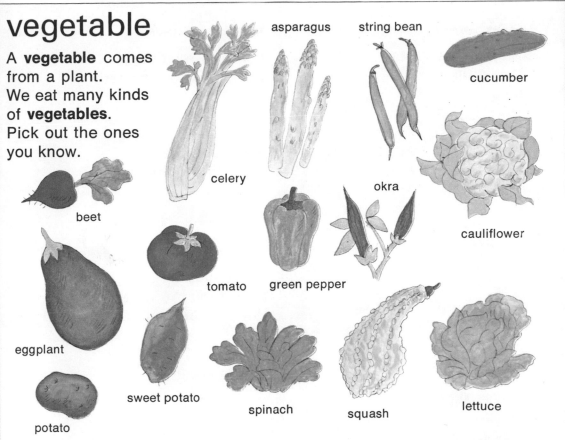

asparagus

string bean

cucumber

celery

okra

cauliflower

beet

tomato

green pepper

eggplant

sweet potato

spinach

squash

lettuce

potato

very

Jan's hair is long. Rita's hair is **very** long.

One building is high. The other is **very** high.

village

A **village** is a small town.

vine

A **vine** is a plant. Some **vines** climb. Some **vines** grow along the ground.

violet

A **violet** is a flower. **Violet** is a color too. The **violets** are **violet**.

violin

A **violin** makes music. A **violin** has four strings. We play **violins** with bows.

visit (visits / visited / visiting)

Aunt Emily has come to **visit**.

Mickey is paying a **visit** to the doctor.

voice

You use your **voice** to talk or sing. Dogs use their **voices** when they bark.

volcano

A **volcano** is one kind of mountain. Hot rock and clouds of smoke sometimes pour from **volcanoes**.

W w

The 23rd letter of the alphabet

wade (wades / waded / wading)

Tom and Martha are **wading**.
They are careful not to **wade** out too far.

wagon

A **wagon** has four wheels.
Toy **wagons** are easy to pull about.

wait (waits / waited / waiting)

Johnny is **waiting** for Chuck.
He will not have to **wait** long.

wake (wakes / waked or woke / waking)

Pal and Howie just **woke** up.

The clock **wakes** Daddy up.

walk (walks / walked / walking)

You **walk** on two feet.
So does a pigeon.

Brad is **walking** Sandy.
He takes Sandy for a long **walk** every day.

wall

There are pictures on one **wall** of the room.

The children built a **wall** around the castle.

want (wants / wanted / wanting)

Do you **want** some milk?
Would you like some milk?

warm (warms / warmed / warming)

Mother is **warming** rolls in the oven.

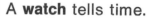

It is **warm** in summer.

wash (washes / washed / washing)

Gwen is **washing** her hands to get ready for dinner.

Mike is putting his socks in the **wash**.

waste (wastes / wasted / wasting)

Somebody forgot to turn off the water.
Water is being **wasted**.

Peg is **wasting** paper.

watch (watches / watched / watching)

Judy is **watching** TV.

Tip **watches** for John to come home.

A **watch** tells time.

water

Water to drink.
Water to wade in.
Water to wash with.
Water to make our gardens grow.
What would we do without **water**?

a b c d e f g h i j k l m

watermelon

A **watermelon** is
a sweet, juicy fruit.

wave (waves / waved / waving)

The baby
is **waving**
good-by
to Keith.
Keith **waves** back.

A big **wave**
is coming in.

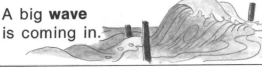

way

Father is showing Jack
the **way** to fly a kite.
Jack wants his kite
to go up a long **way**.

The mother duck leads
the **way**.

wear (wears / wore / wearing)

Edith is **wearing**
her new poncho.

Jody **wore** a hole
in one shoe.

weather

What kind of **weather**
do you like best?

Wednesday

Wednesday is a day
of the week.
Wednesday comes
after Tuesday.

weed

A **weed** is a plant
growing where
we do not want it.
Some **weeds** have
pretty flowers.

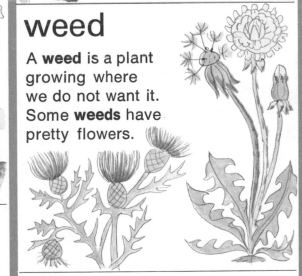

week

Seven days make a **week**.
What day is today?
What day is a **week** from today?
Daddy's vacation lasted
three **weeks**.

weigh (weighs / weighed / weighing)

Jake is getting
weighed.
Do you think Frank
weighs as much
as Jake?

well

Sally was sick.
Now she is **well** again.
Can you do what Sally
is doing as **well** as
she can?

well

Water comes
from this **well**.

We get oil
from this kind of **well**.

west

Dick is looking north.
His left hand
is pointing **west**.
The sun sets
in the **west**.

n o p q r s t u v **w** x y z

wet

Andy and Alice and Skipper are **wet**. They got **wet** in the rain.

whale

A **whale** is the biggest animal there is. **Whales** live in the sea.

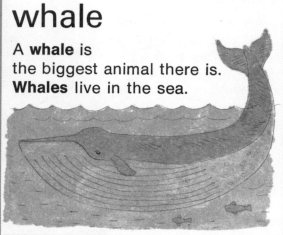

what

Many questions start with **what**. **What** time is it? **What** is your name?

wheat

Wheat is a grain. **Wheat** makes good flour for bread and rolls and cake and cookies.

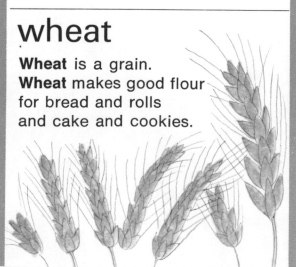

wheel

A **wheel** turns around and around. Cars have **wheels**. Bicycles have **wheels**. Turn back to page 59 and look for **wheels**.

wheelbarrow

A **wheelbarrow** helps us move heavy loads.

when

Many questions start with **when**. **When** did you get up today? **When** will supper be ready?

where

Many questions start with **where**. **Where** do you live? **Where** are the baby chickens? **Where** is the caterpillar?

which

Many questions start with **which**. **Which** line is longest? **Which** bug is biggest?

whisper (whispers / whispered / whispering)

Cathy is **whispering** to her mother. Nobody but her mother can hear her.

whistle (whistles / whistled / whistling)

Jimmy is **whistling** because he is happy. Can you **whistle**?

Danny made one of these **whistles**. Which **whistle** is it?

white

Snow is **white**.

The lily is **white**.

The owl is **white**.

who

Many questions start with **who**.
Who is it?
Who lives next door?

whole

Sue ate a **whole** cupcake.
She ate all of it.
Could you eat
a **whole** watermelon?

why

Many questions start with **why**.
Why does it get dark at night?
Why can't an ostrich fly?

wide

Is the street you live on
a **wide** one?
Is it far from one side
to the other?

The hippopotamus has
its mouth **wide** open.
How **wide** can you open
yours?

wild

These are **wild** animals.
They find
their own food.

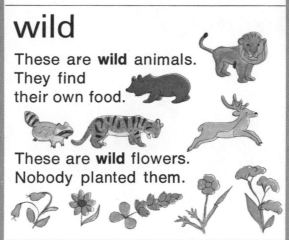

These are **wild** flowers.
Nobody planted them.

win (wins / won / winning)

Barney is **winning**.
He will come in first.
Barney **won**
the first game too.

wind

The **wind** is blowing.
You cannot see
the **wind,** but you can see
what the **wind** does.

wind (winds / wound / winding)

The toy bear dances
if you **wind** it.

Carlotta **wound**
the string into a ball.

window

The **window**
is open.
Windows let in
light and air.

wing

A bird has two **wings**.

A butterfly has four.

One **wing**
of the toy airplane
is broken.

winter

Is it spring
in the picture?
Is it summer?
Is it fall?
Is it **winter**?

wipe (wipes / wiped / wiping)

Karen is **wiping**
her hands on the towel.

Toby just **wiped** his.
Did he wash them clean?

n o p q r s t u v **w** x y z

wire

A **wire** is stronger
than a string.
Wires are metal.

wish (wishes / wished / wishing)

Do you **wish** you could go
to the moon?
Do you want to go
to the moon?

Ricky **wished** for
a bicycle.
His **wish** came true.

witch

There are **witches**
in some fairy stories.
At Halloween we see
pictures of **witches**.

with

Mother took Cindy
with her to the store.

Tuffy is fighting
with Spot.

without

The donkey looks funny
without a tail.

wolf (wolves)

A **wolf** looks like
a big dog.
Wolves are
wild animals.

woman (women)

Dora will be a **woman**
when she grows up.
Mothers are **women**.
These **women**
are having lunch.

wonder (wonders / wondered / wondering)

Peggy **wonders**
which hand to pick.

wonderful

Billy and Jean
think a circus is
wonderful.

wood

All these things
are made of **wood**.
Wood comes from trees.

woods

The baby bears live
in the **woods**.

woodpecker

A **woodpecker** is a bird.
Woodpeckers make holes
in wood
with their bills.
They go rat-a-tat-tat.

wool

Wool comes from sheep.
Things made out of **wool**
are warm.

word

We talk with **words**.
We write with **words**.

a b c d e f g h i j k l m

work (works / worked / working)

All these people are **working**. People do many different kinds of **work**.

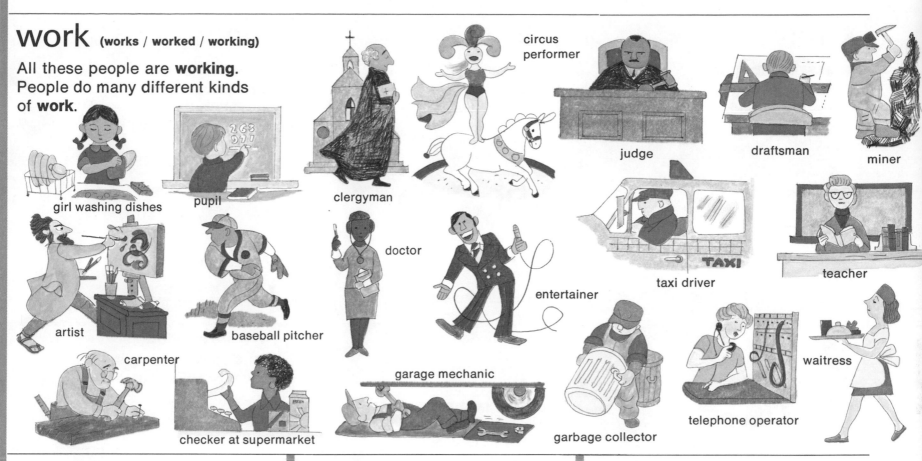

circus performer

judge

draftsman

miner

clergyman

girl washing dishes

pupil

doctor

entertainer

taxi driver

teacher

artist

baseball pitcher

carpenter

garage mechanic

garbage collector

telephone operator

waitress

checker at supermarket

world

There are many people in the **world**. There are many people on the earth.

worm

A **worm** is an animal. **Worms** have no legs.

clamworm

ornate worm

earthworm

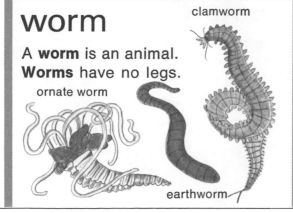

wrap (wraps / wrapped / wrapping)

Joy is **wrapping** Christmas presents. Liz has **wrapped** hers.

wrist

Touch one of your **wrists**. Wave good-by. Did you bend your **wrist**?

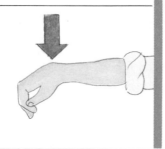

write (writes / wrote / writing)

Carl **writes** well.

Sally **wrote** her name in her new book.

wrong

Jill put the **wrong** shoe on one foot. How can you tell?

n o p q r s t u v **w** x y z

X x

The 24th letter of the alphabet

Xmas

Xmas is another way of writing Christmas.

X ray

Peter hurt his leg. The doctor took an **X ray** of it. The **X ray** showed that a bone was broken.

xylophone

A **xylophone** makes music. We play **xylophones** with little hammers.

Y y

The 25th letter of the alphabet

yak

A **yak** is an animal with long hair. Their hair keeps **yaks** warm.

yard

A **yard** tells how long. A **yard** is the same as 36 inches.

The little **yard** has pretty flowers in it. At school there is a big **yard** to play in.

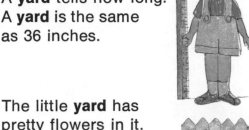

yarn

Sweaters are made of **yarn**. So are caps and scarfs for winter.

The kitten has Mother's ball of **yarn**!

year

A **year** is twelve months long. We tell how old we are in **years**.

yell (yell / yelled / yelling)

Barbara is **yelling** at Albert. She wants her doll back. Do you ever **yell**?

yellow

Yellow is a color.

Here are a **yellow** cat and a **yellow** dress and a **yellow** buttercup.

yes

Do ducks quack?

Is water wet?

Can fish swim? The answers are all **yes**.

yesterday

Yesterday is the day before today. If today is Monday, what was **yesterday**?

a b c d e f g h i j k l m

112

yet

Is Pat ready **yet**?
No, he hasn't put
his coat on **yet**.
Up to now he hasn't
put it on.

yolk

An egg has a **yolk**.
The **yolk** is yellow.

young

All these animals are
young.
They are not very old.

yo-yo

Caroline is playing
with a **yo-yo**.
Yo-yos go up and down
on strings.

Z z

The 26th letter of the alphabet

zebra

A **zebra** has stripes.
Zebras are very much
like horses.

zero

Zero tells how many.
It means none at all.
We use two **zeros**
to write 100.
What letter does
a **zero** look like?

zinnia

A **zinnia** is a flower.
Zinnias come
in many pretty colors.

zipper

The jacket fastens
with a **zipper**.
The boots have **zippers**.
Do you have any clothes
with **zippers**?

zoo

A **zoo** is a kind of park.
There are many animals
to see in **zoos**.
Some of the animals
come from far **away**.

elephant

flamingo

monkey

giraffe

rhinoceros

buffalo

lion

polar bear

antelope

sea lion

tiger

n o p q r s t u v w x y z

To Parents and Teachers

The New Golden Dictionary invites three- to seven-year-olds to explore their own world of words. With this dictionary as a map and you as a traveling companion, a child will travel far along the road to making hundreds of happy discoveries.

Along with the fun, he'll be moving ahead in language learning. The dictionary is ready to help in a variety of ways:

To stimulate an interest in words. Three- and four-year olds will enjoy pointing to a picture and calling out the word it illustrates. Children in the early years of school will take pride in recognizing the printed words. Experiences with the words and word games in this dictionary will lead most children to decide that words can be quite exciting.

To help with beginning reading. The close relationship between pictures and words in this dictionary has special value in making children aware that words stand for objects and ideas. The defining sentences aid in building reading readiness as preschoolers read along with you, and the sentences give primary-graders satisfying practice in reading by themselves.

To help with writing and speaking. Children will find in this dictionary most of the words needed for the stories they tell and write. Here's how-to-spell-it help, plus an easy way to check on word meanings. The dictionary sentences provide models of standard, informal English — valuable in encouraging good usage habits and developing sensitivity to language patterns.

To start the dictionary habit growing. With this dictionary youngsters can get off to a good start in the skills that make dictionary use rewarding. They learn to find words in an alphabetical arrangement, to use sentences and pictures to arrive at word meanings, to discover that a word may have more than one meaning. Most important, perhaps, children who enjoy using this dictionary are acquiring a friendly feeling for dictionaries in general.

The Words

Words in *The New Golden Dictionary* were chosen on the basis of their familiarity and usefulness to today's children. Here are words they hear on television, use in everyday conversation, meet in schoolbooks prepared for the early years. Observation of children's speech was a guide to the selection of words. The word list was also checked against a wide variety of children's books.

In this dictionary 1262 words are defined. Along with these entry words, 880 inflected forms are shown. Other important additions to the basic vocabulary are words that are illustrated and grouped under entry words for such categories as *animals, buildings, space,* and *work.* For example, under *animals,* there are pictures of 32 creatures, among them, *beaver, clam, spider, butterfly, koala,* and *lizard.* Some of the words that illustrate categories are also used as separate entry words, but over 450 are used only under the category entries, bringing the total word count to approximately 2600.

The New Golden Dictionary is a real dictionary with a well-rounded vocabulary. The word list is not limited to concrete nouns, though plenty of these useful naming words are included. There are words for ideas, too, like *brave* and *time.* There are verbs that help a child describe his active world, adjectives and adverbs frequently used by youngsters, structure words like *and, but, from* and *to.* As in dictionaries for adults, all the words are arranged in a single alphabetical list.

The Illustrations

More than 2000 lively illustrations are ready to lead youngsters into this dictionary and to keep them coming back again and again. The pictures function as meaning-givers. With a great many of the entries, a child can look at the picture and know immediately what the entry word is and what it means.

In many cases, where a single picture might result in misconceptions about a word, several illustrations are used. See, for instance, the entries *bring* and *five.* Multiple illustrations are also used to show various meanings for a word, as in *bulb.* In some cases where the entry word is not a concrete noun, the illustration is made somewhat complex so as not to focus on one object and thus give a wrong clue. See *along,* for example.

The pictures stay close to the child's experience. Many have a touch of humor; all reflect keen understanding of the child and his world. A broad range of environments — urban, suburban, rural — is represented, as are many kinds of people. Any child is sure to find a large number of pictures with which he can identify.

The Sentences

Sentences work with the illustrations to help children understand the meanings of the entry words. Sometimes a word is directly defined —"A *pebble* is a small, smooth stone." Or the meaning is given by restating an idea —"The red boots *belong* to George. They are George's boots." In many entries the way the word is used reveals its meaning —"Chris is *laughing* at something funny." In still others, sentences point up the meaning shown in the picture —"This man has a red *beard.*"

In constructing the sentences, special attention was given to the normal speech patterns of children and to the vocabulary at their command. Except for proper names and such very common words as *a, the, this, you, is* and *here,* 99 percent of the words used in the sentences appear also as entry words or in the category-word groups.

Child Involvement

You have doubtless noticed that a great many sentences in *The New Golden Dictionary* include children's names. The object, of course, is to give as many children as possible the pleasure of finding their own names or their friends' names in this book.

Many sentences also invite the young dictionary user to take part in the action. *"Bend* down and touch your toes," "Find (in the picture) *one* owl and *one* grasshopper and *one* jar of honey," "When is your *birthday?"* are samples of the encouragement given a youngster to become personally involved in word meanings.

Dictionary Games

The games and activities described on the following pages are pleasant ways for children to participate in still more dictionary fun and learning. A look at the titles will suggest the variety of good times in store for the players who, by using the games, will soon be learning to name and classify things, identify sounds and letters, utilize the alphabet, look up words in the dictionary.

Instructions for each game are addressed to you, and in most cases, tell how to play it with one child. Many of the games can be easily adapted for use by groups of children or by one youngster playing alone.

Dictionary Games

Find the Real One

In THE NEW GOLDEN DICTIONARY, choose a picture of something the child can find in the room — a book, a chair, a dog, a lamp, or the like. Show the child the picture and ask, "What is this a picture of?" When he has named the object, ask "Can you find a real one like it?" He then looks for and points out an object that matches the one in the picture.

Name the Picture

Open the dictionary to page 5 and ask the child if he can find a picture of an airplane on this page. Of course he can. Then point to the entry word for the picture and ask, "What do you suppose this word says? . . . That's right, this word says air-plane."

Any entry word that names something and has a picture in the dictionary works well for this activity.

Reader's Choice

Select a page of the dictionary that displays pictures of objects your youngster is familiar with — perhaps dog, doll, doughnut. The child points to a picture he chooses and asks you, "What is this a picture of?" You give him the word and ask, "Am I right?" If the child has another word in mind, such as puppy instead of dog, show him the entry for puppy and help him compare pictures and words.

Something Good to Eat

For another version of "Name the Picture," turn to a dictionary page that includes a word for a kind of food and say, "Find a picture of something good to eat . . . What do you call it? . . . What do you think this word says?"

Something to eat with, something to wear, something to ride in also make good topics for this game.

Read Along

You and your child can have good times reading together from THE NEW GOLDEN DICTIONARY. Let the child choose entries he would like you to read to him. As you read the sentences, pause when you come to the entry word and let the child supply this word.

What Did We See Today?

After a trip to the supermarket with your preschooler, use THE NEW GOLDEN DICTIONARY for a remembering game. Recall together, and look up the entries for things seen on the way — street, stop sign, car, bus, boy, bicycle, ending up with super-market. Then turn to the entry for vegetables and say, "There are some things here we saw at the supermarket. Let's see how many we can find." Hunt under fruit, meat, and food too.

Acting Out Words

With the dictionary open to an action word like dance, hop, or smile, invite the child to look at the word and its picture. "What do you think this word is? Show how you do what the word says." The child says the word and shows how he dances or hops or smiles.

Other words that are fun to act out include crawl, jump, run, skip, whisper, whistle. Child can also pantomime the action expressed in words like carry, catch, drive, pull, throw, and wipe.

Make a Body Chart

Have the child lie down on a length of wrapping paper. Trace around him. Names for parts of the body are added — either by you or the child — to this outline as the child finds them in his dictionary and shows where they belong on the chart. The search might begin in the F section of the dictionary, where the child finds illustrated entries for face, finger, foot, and forehead. The letter E is good, too, with ear, elbow, and eye.

The youngster can add arms, legs, mouth, and so on to his body chart as soon as he finds the words for them in his dictionary. If he needs help, steer him to the appropriate pages. Pictures will help him take it from there.

Shopping Game

From the alphabet shown at the bottom of his NEW GOLDEN DICTIONARY pages, the child chooses a letter as "territory" for a pretend trip to a grocery store. Suppose he chooses the letter P. Open the dictionary to the P's and let the child look for pictures of things he might find in a grocery store — for example, peach, peanut, pickles, popcorn, potato, pumpkin. He must name the item pictured before pretending to buy it. And no fair trying to buy a pony in a grocery store!

Dictionary shopping trips might also be taken to a toy store, a clothing store, or a pet shop.

Sound Alikes

The child follows along as you read aloud a column of entry words; he then says the words with you. Ask, "Can you hear that every one of these words begins with the same sound? . . . Can you think of any other words that begin like these words?" Help the child look in the dictionary for his suggested words, letting him see, should he find them, that their begin-nings look, as well as sound, alike.

Words beginning with b, d, f, m, or v are good starters for this game. Stay away from c, g, k, w, and any other letters that do not always have the same sound at the beginning of a word.

Wrong Word

Read to the child a string of words from a dictionary page, putting in one word that doesn't belong there. For example: baby, back, bad, bag, bake, duck, ball, balloon. Say, "One word doesn't belong in this list because it doesn't begin the same way the other words begin. Can you tell which word doesn't belong?" The child can check his answer by looking at the dictionary page from which you read and making sure that the "wrong" word — in this case duck — is not there. Then guide him to page 31, on which duck is entered, and ask him to point to the letter that duck begins with.

Poem About Me

For Jimmies and Janes, J is the most important letter of the alphabet; for Annes and Andrews, A gets the vote. To celebrate the letter that appears at the beginning of your child's name, try making up a rhyme using his name and one or two entries from THE NEW GOLDEN DICTIONARY. For example:

The letter E	Sandwich and Saturday
Stands for elevator	Start with S,
And a boy named Ed	And so does Sarah,
And escalator.	As you can guess.

Alphabet Song

A B C D E F G H I J K L M N O P

Q R S T U and V W X and Y and Z

The child points to each letter of the alphabet shown on his *NEW GOLDEN DICTIONARY* pages as he sings the name of the letter. Start by having him sing and point along with you. Once learned, this game gives him a happy way to entertain himself.

Furniture Mover

Draw a simple floor plan for three or four rooms in an imaginary house or apartment and let the child furnish them with words he finds in his *NEW GOLDEN DICTIONARY*. The dictionary entry for *furniture* pictures a number of items he can sort out according to the rooms in which he thinks they belong. When he has decided what goes where, print the words on the floor plan. Then turn to other dictionary pages on which he'll find more furnishings for his rooms. For example:

Living room — clock, piano, picture, television
Bedroom — crib, lamp, mirror, pillow
Kitchen — cupboard, refrigerator, sink, stove

Alphabet Scrapbook

On a shopping trip let your child choose a scrapbook or notebook for his own alphabet book. Print an alphabet letter in both the capital and small forms in the top lefthand corner of each page. Or paste on the pages letters cut from newspaper headlines. On the page with the letter that starts the child's name, let him paste his picture. His name becomes the *key word* for that letter. The other 25 key words he will choose over a period of time from his *NEW GOLDEN DICTIONARY*. Have him search through magazines and catalogs for a picture to illustrate each key word chosen and paste it on the appropriate page of the alphabet scrapbook.

Sightseeing

A game similar to "My father owns a grocery store, and he sells ...." begins as you tell your child, "We're going for a pretend walk, and we'll see a *mailbox*," (or *dandelion* or *rooster,* or an object beginning with any other letter that always sounds the same at the beginning of a word). "Can you think of something else we might see whose beginning sounds like the beginning of *mailbox*. After the child suggests a word (*man,* perhaps), he tries to find it in the dictionary, which you open for him to the appropriate section. Point out that all the words in the section look alike, as well as sound alike, at the beginning. Find in the section other things he might have seen on the pretend walk.

Grandma Is Filling Her Shopping Bag

For a variation on the sightseeing game, start with the sentence "Grandma is filling her shopping bag with *peanuts*," (or *newspapers* or *feathers* or *lemons*). Some remarkably bulky objects may get into the bag.

Instead of using words that all begin with the same letter, have the child fill grandma's shopping bag with 26 objects, starting with one for *A* and continuing with one for each letter through *Z*. Let him turn through the dictionary from front to back to get any help he needs. School-age children can play this game together.

Alphabet Days

Any day can be a good time to celebrate a letter of the alphabet. First, blindfold the child and let him point to a letter of the alphabet in his dictionary. That letter becomes the letter of the day. Here are some ways he can celebrate almost any letter:

Wear a big paper button with the letter crayoned on it. If the child's name begins with the letter of the day, he wears a headband too. The headband can be a ribbon to which you staple a paper medallion displaying the child's name.

Make up a "silly saying," using words that begin with the letter. Examples: "A bird on the beach bought a bee for his breakfast"; "Vera visited a volcano on Valentine's Day." *THE NEW GOLDEN DICTIONARY* will help the child think of words to use in the sayings.

Sing the Alphabet Song, stopping at the letter of the day.

Add an animal to an Alphabet Zoo. The zoo can be a sheet of brown wrapping paper. With the dictionary opened to the letter of the day, the child looks for a picture of an animal. If he finds one, he says its name and draws its picture on the paper zoo. Its name can be printed beside the picture. Animal names can be found for most letters — *alligator, butterfly, camel, donkey, elephant, frog, goat,* and so on. Stay out of the zoo for letters *N, Q, U, V,* and *X*.

Model the letter in clay. Show child how to make a roll of modeling clay he can bend to look like the capital letter he sees in his dictionary.

You can add to Alphabet-Day fun with a variety of activities for each letter. Here are a few examples:

On *A*-Day:

Make and wear an *A*-Day *apron.* It can be made of newspaper or a paper bag and labeled with a big *A* in finger paint or thick marking pencil. Thread a piece of yarn or ribbon through holes in the top of the apron to tie around the waist.

Be an *acrobat.* The youngster tries somersaults, headstands, cartwheels, and the like.

On *J*-Day:

See how far you can *jump.*

Make yourself a *jelly* sandwich.

Play a *joke* on someone.

Watch for a *jet plane* in the sky.

On *M*-Day:

Hunt for *machines* in your house. The pictures in the dictionary under *machines* will suggest things to look for.

March across the room.

Drink an extra glass of *milk.*

On *Y*-Day:

Draw a picture of something *yellow.* It might be a banana, a piece of cheese, a canary, a daffodil, the sun, etc.

Tell what happened *yesterday.* The happenings can be as simple as having soup for lunch or playing with the puppy.

Play with a *yo-yo.*

File Fun

Make a collection of simple pictures — airplane, balloon, candy, and so on — one for each letter of the alphabet. Give your child a few of these pictures at a time and show him how to file them in his alphabet scrapbook. Have him say the names of key pictures in his scrapbook to help him decide where each picture belongs: For example, he should put a balloon picture on the page with a picture whose name begins with the *b* sound — perhaps baby. Help him with any names beginning with letters that vary in sound.

To keep this game easy, group together for the child's use pictures whose names fall at the beginning of the alphabet (A-G), in the middle (H-P), or at the end (Q-Z). Steer the child to the comparable part of his scrapbook.

Match the Letters

Make 52 cards by cutting 3 inch by 5 inch file cards in half. On 26 cards print or paste the letters of the alphabet in capital letters, one to each card. On the other 26 cards print or paste the letters of the alphabet in small letters, one to each card.

Have the child lay out the capital cards face up. Then have him match the small letters with the capitals. Of course he may consult the dictionary.

This activity can be made into a good game for from two to five children. To play the game put the cards face down in two bowls, the capitals in one bowl and the small letters in the other. Each player draws five cards with capitals and puts them right side up in front of him. Then the players take turns drawing small letters. If the letter a player draws matches one of his capitals, he puts it beside the capital. If not, without letting anyone see it, he returns it, face down, to the bowl. The player wins who first has all his capitals matched with small letters.

Keep the 52 cards for other games.

Rhyme Time

Let the child pick an entry on a dictionary page of his choice; perhaps he settles on goat. He says to you, "Rhyme time, what's the rhyme?" Suppose you think of coat as a rhyme for goat; instead of saying coat aloud, turn to the page of the dictionary on which the word coat appears. When the child finds it, he may pick another rhyme-time entry.

If the child asks you for a rhyme for a word like giraffe or Halloween, tell him you give up, and have him choose another word.

Letter Lineup

Use the set of alphabet cards made for "Match the Letters." Give the capital cards A through G to your child and let him arrange them in alphabetical order, using the alphabet at the bottom of THE NEW GOLDEN DICTIONARY pages as a guide. Follow on other days with H through P and with Q through Z. Finally, let him arrange the whole alphabet at once. Repeat with small letters.

Alphabet Jump Rope

Instead of the verses children often chant as they jump rope, a child can say the alphabet, one letter for each jump. When he forgets the next letter or says one out of order, stop him and have him check the alphabet in his dictionary before he starts to jump again. The object, of course, is to get all the way from A to Z without stopping.

Two children can play this game together, with one child watching the alphabet in the dictionary while the other jumps. When the jumper makes a mistake, the two trade places.

Before and After

The youngster uses the alphabet in his NEW GOLDEN DICTIONARY to answer such questions as: "What letter comes right after C in the alphabet?" "What letter comes just before N?" "What letter comes between R and T?" The child points to the letter and says its name.

Rhyming Riddles

Open THE NEW GOLDEN DICTIONARY to any pair of pages and ask your child a rhyming riddle about one of the entry words shown there. A riddle about plate, for instance, could go like this: "Find a picture of something we put food on. Its name rhymes with late. What is the word?"

For a child who knows the alphabet letters and related sounds, start with the dictionary closed. Say, for example, "Find the name of something that you could take a ride in. Its name begins with b and rhymes with float."

Back Up

When a child can point in his dictionary to each letter of the alphabet as he says, or sings, its name, let him try reading the alphabet backwards. To start: "Point to the last letter of the alphabet in your dictionary and say its name . . . Now the letter just before the last letter . . . Now the letter before that . . . Let's see how quickly you can back up from Z to Q . . . from P to H . . . from G to A."

What's the First Letter?

Show the child some such list as this:

_each, _arachute, _enny, _izza

Tell him that the first letter of each of these words is the same. If he needs a clue, show him pictures of some familiar objects the names of which begin with p — maybe pear and pencil. When he thinks he knows what the letter is, help him check the four words in his dictionary.

Dictionary-opening Game

Tell the child, "I'm going to call out a letter, and you open your dictionary to a page where there are words beginning with that letter. I'll count to see how quickly you find it. Try to think where the letter is in the alphabet." Call the letter A first . . . then Z . . . then M (at the middle of the dictionary). Continue with other letters. After five or six letters are called, call the same letters over again to let the child try to break his record.

Alphabet Picture

Copy the pattern of alphabet letters and the circles and lines shown below on a large unlined sheet of paper. Show the child the starting point — the dot at A — and tell him to draw a line from A to B, from B to C, and so on all the way to Z. When he has finished he will have a picture. (It will be a picture of a steamship, but let him find this out for himself.)

Alphabet-picture pattern:

The following drawing shows the puzzle picture with colored lines added to show how it would appear when the child connects the dots.

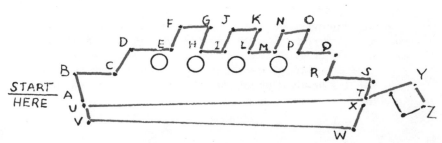

117

Looking for Vowels

From the letters you've cut from headlines or printed on cards, help the child pick out *a, e, i, o, u,* and *y.* Tell him that every word in his dictionary has at least one of these letters in it. Open the dictionary to the first page of *B*'s and ask the child to find a word with three *a*'s in it. Help him run his finger down the page till he finds *banana.* Tell him there is a word in the *B*'s that has an *a* and an *e* and an *i* and two *u*'s in it. The word means "very pretty." Look with him till he finds *beautiful.* This activity can go on and on.

Who Likes What?

Using your name (probably Mommy to your child) and your child's name, play this initial-letter game. Say, Mommy likes a *mirror,*" (or *Monday* or *moonlight),* and locate the entry in THE NEW GOLDEN DICTIONARY. Then continue, using the child's name: "What does...................like?" Perhaps the child can find the word he wants, unassisted, of you remind him that he'll find what he is looking for among the words that start like his name. Continue, taking turns.

For additional "Who Likes What" possibilities, introduce the names of other family members or friends. This game also works well for a group of more than two.

Match the Words

Print on 3 inch by 5 inch cards a half-dozen words you and your child have explored in one section of THE NEW GOLDEN DICTIONARY — perhaps *farm, feather, fish, fire engine, flashlight, frog.* Open the dictionary to the *F*'s and have the child match the words on the cards to entry words in the book. When the child locates a word in the dictionary, the picture helps him read it.

This game is easiest when the words you put on cards don't look too much alike. For example, a child can see that *feather* is longer than *farm,* that *fish* has a tall letter at the end and *farm* doesn't. On the other hand, he might have trouble seeing the difference between *fog* and *frog.*

Put Them in Order

Help the youngster to think of four words, each beginning with a different letter. Print the words, one on each of four small pieces of paper. Say, "Look at the letters these words start with. Which of these letters is nearest the beginning of the alphabet? Let's put the word that begins with that letter first on our list . . . Now move your finger across the alphabet in your dictionary till you come to the next letter that one of our words starts with. We'll put that word next in our list. . . ." Continue until the four words are listed in alphabetical order. When the child sees how to alphabetize, he'll enjoy doing it with many short lists of words. Here are a few four-word lists you might give him:

truck	toy	yellow	dog
airplane	ball	green	cat
car	doll	blue	zebra
ship	sled	red	monkey

How Fast Can You Find the Word?

For a youngster who can read, play the "Dictionary-opening Game" by calling out words instead of letters. Count slowly while he looks for the word in his NEW GOLDEN DICTIONARY and put down the number you've reached when he finds the word. The child then tries to beat his own record for speedy word-finding.

Fill the Slot

Give the child a sentence in which a word is missing. For example: The.........................ate hungrily. Say, "Turn to the *D*'s in your dictionary and see how many words you can find that make sense in this sentence." The youngster can come up with *daughter, dentist, doctor, dog, donkey, duck,* and *dwarf.* Then let him choose another letter in his NEW GOLDEN DICTIONARY — any letter except *V* or *X* — and find other words to fill the slot.

Here are some more sentences to use in this game:

The...................lay on the ground. (Choose any letter.)

The dog was........................ (Letters *A, B, H, L, S, T,* and *W* work well with this one.)

Jim like to........................... (Try the letters *C, D, H, P, R, S,* and *W.*)

a, e, i, o, u

Suggest to the child that he look at THE NEW GOLDEN DICTIONARY entries beginning with b and ask him to find the first word in which *b* is followed by *a* . . . by *e* . . . by *i* . . . by *o* . . . by *u.* For *b* he can come up with *baby, beach, bicycle, board, bubble.* For *c* the list would be *cabbage, cent, circle, coal, cup.* This activity also works well for entries beginning with *d, f, h, l, m, n, p, r, s,* and *t.*

Animals, People, and Things

When a child can read a little, let him try classifying some dictionary entries as animals, people, and things. Pick a page that has at least one of each — page 22, for instance. Say, "Can you find any words for animals on this page?" The youngster will find *chipmunk;* he may know that *chicken* is an animal too. Next ask him to look for words for people; on this page he'll find *child.* Then let him hunt for names of things — *cherry, chest, chimney,* and others.

After a child becomes good at this game, he may enjoy running his finger down the columns of entries and identifying words for animals, people, and things as he comes to them. In the *K*'s, for instance, he might say, "Kangaroo, animals," "Key, things," "King, people," and so on,

Alphabetical Puzzle

Give the child a string of words that will make a sentence when he puts them in alphabetical order. For example:

wheels   has   a   two   bicycle

The string of words becomes, with capital and period:

A bicycle has two wheels.

Using his dictionary, when necessary, to keep the alphabetical order straight, the youngster can have fun unscrambling word strings like these:

on   apples   trees   grow

have   trunks   elephants   long

ran   girls   four   upstairs

book   many   pictures   Anne's   has

whistle   to   Billy   learned   yesterday

giraffe   a   wall   looked   the   over

picked   yellow   zinnias   a   seven   girl

jump   can   puddles   any   over   boy